WOKE

Woke

A Guide to Social Justice

Titania McGrath

CONSTABLE

CONSTABLE

First published in Great Britain in 2019 by Constable

5 7 9 10 8 6

A CIP catalogue record for this book
is available from the British Library.

ISBN: 978-1-47213-084-6 (hardback)

Typeset in Sabon LT by Hewer Text UK Ltd, Edinburgh
Printed and bound in Great Britain by Clays Ltd, Elcograf S.p.A.

Papers used by Constable are from well-managed
forests and other responsible sources.

MIX
Paper from
responsible sources
FSC® C104740
www.fsc.org

Constable
An imprint of
Little, Brown Book Group
Carmelite House
50 Victoria Embankment
London EC4Y 0DZ

An Hachette UK Company
www.hachette.co.uk

www.littlebrown.co.uk

Only through hardship, sacrifice and militant action can freedom be won.

Nelson Mandela

It's not a smile; it's a lid on a scream.

Bet Lynch

My poetry is uncompromising
My instincts are profound.
I am feared by the powerful.
I am adored by the oppressed.
I am truth.
I am Titania McGrath.

Titania McGrath

Contents

Introduction

God *is a black Jewish lesbian.*
Derek Jarman

I was born woke. My wokeness is innate. It flows
through me like a magical elixir, keeping my soul
purged and poised for the fight. In many ways, I
am a modern-day Joan of Arc: indomitable, preco-
cious, fluent in French.

Strangers often compliment me on my unwavering
sense of social justice. 'Titania,' they say, 'we've only
just met, but you strike me as one whose very existence embodies the interconnected virtues of courage
and truth.' This kind of thing happens to me almost
every day.

Allow me to formally introduce myself. My name is
Titania Gethsemane McGrath. I am a radical intersectionalist poet committed to feminism, social justice
and armed peaceful protest.

Over the past few years I have become a formidable
presence on the live slam-poetry scene. For those of
you who are unfamiliar with slam, it's like regular

poetry but with extra pauses. And there's usually a lactose-free buffet at the end.

I often perform at arts festivals, deconsecrated churches and lesbian spiritual retreats. I have written over five thousand poems, a selection of which are included in this volume. I am particularly fond of 'How to Prod a Shepherd', a piece dedicated to my Uncle Asbjørn, the only man I have ever loved. May he rest in peace when he dies.

There are moments when the extent of my own talent frightens me. Sometimes, when I read my work, I cannot but help come to the conclusion that I am the only living artist worthy of note. I have that rare ability to take a linguistic scalpel to the cancerous bigotry of modern Western culture.

As a millennial icon on the forefront of online activism, I am uniquely placed to guide you through the often bewildering array of concepts that constitute contemporary 'wokeness'. To put it bluntly, I am a much better person than you.

This isn't arrogance. I'd go so far as to say it's a curse to be so gifted. I'd much rather be mediocre like everyone else.

For too long the battle for social justice has been waged by middle-class hipsters, the kind who shop at Urban Outfitters and think that beard oil is a sensible investment. But being woke is actually much easier than people think. Anyone can be an activist. By simply adding a rainbow flag to your Facebook profile, or calling out an elderly person who doesn't understand what 'non-binary' means, you can change the world for the better. Indeed, social media has now made it possible to show how virtuous you are without having to do anything at all.

Activists such as myself are spearheading a new culture war, sniffing out prejudice like valiant blood-hounds of righteousness, courageously snapping at the heels of injustice. To give a tangible example of our achievements, consider how the definition of the word 'Nazi' has been successfully broadened to include anyone who voted for Brexit, has ever considered supporting the Conservative Party or who refuses to take the *Guardian* seriously. Although this is a great victory for the progressive cause, it does mean that there are now more Nazis living in modern Britain than even existed in 1930s Germany. This makes *Woke: A Guide to Social Justice* not only timely, but essential.

A male could not have written this book. Males can never achieve peak wokeness due to their fundamentally toxic masculinity. They fear the power of the yoni, the primal cadence of the menstrual flow. Women are celestial goddesses, blood-sisters of the sacred moon witch.

I am a teller of truths, a slayer of patriarchs, a fearless metaphysician. I teabag the foes of justice with a gender-neutral scrotum. I suckle the babes of hope with my sinewy teats of equality.

If you are reading this, it is likely that you suffer from an inability to keep up with modern trends. I am here to guide you through the minefields of social justice, to remodel you into a more appealing version of yourself. Imagine me as a potter in her workshop, and yourself as a malformed lump of clay.

If you are willing, I can shape your destiny.

My Struggle

Forgive, but don't forget, girl, keep ya head up.
Tupac Shakur

I may have been born woke, but it was a distinctly unwoke world into which I emerged. This is why I have always been so radical. My first act as a baby was to piss onto the obstetrician. I didn't cry at all, which apparently caused some alarm. The nurse slapped me to see if a reaction could be stimulated. I remained defiant.

I was the only child of two barristers. I learnt early on that my private education and frequent family holidays to Montenegro and the Maldives were merely a ruse by which my parents could distract me from my oppression.

My infant years were beset with psychological trauma, which should come as no great surprise. To be born into a heteronormative patriarchal white supremacist world can be a strain on anyone's psyche, particularly for a feminist toddler who is expected to sit still and not complain.

I had been breastfed for the first six months of my life. Did my mother not realise that I was a vegan? Did she even care? Either way, this was abuse.

Before I was even out of the crib I was self-harming with my nappy pin. By the age of four, I was suffering from both anorexia and chronic overeating. When these two conditions occur simultaneously it can be difficult to spot, because the victim ends up eating a regular amount of food on a consistent basis.

But I was bleeding inside. My insides were literally full of blood.

After I enrolled at my local nursery I decided to identify as genderqueer. I instinctively knew that I must resist what Laurie Penny has described as 'the disaster of heterosexuality'. I was light years ahead of my time, because at that point the term 'genderqueer' didn't even exist. The teachers had never heard of a gender-neutral toilet, so my demands were met with blank stares. Little wonder, then, that I have ended up with a severe case of self-diagnosed post-traumatic stress disorder.

I have always been playful with language. I remember lunches at infant school where I would use the Alphabetti Spaghetti to spell out creative synonyms for 'vulva'. Even at the tender age of five, I was keen to demystify the commonplace societal prejudices against the female reproductive system.

As I got older I excelled at all academic subjects, except for biology, physics, chemistry, economics, history, religious studies, computing and mathematics. I quickly realised that it was not due to 'failure' on my part, but rather that these fields of study are patriarchal constructs that perpetuate white privilege. My adolescent self was intuitively mistrustful; my low grades were doubtless a valiant act of subconscious self-sabotage.

As Professor Rochelle Gutiérrez from the University of Illinois has pointed out, 'on many levels, mathematics itself operates as Whiteness'. Indeed, the Ku Klux Klan were once known to set fire to plus signs in order to intimidate their victims.

Besides, Pythagoras fingered kids.

It was at school that my poetical predispositions found something to rail against. A cishet male English teacher known as Mr Gourlay attempted to teach us one of Wordsworth's sonnets. I think it was about a bridge or something. Everything about it – the forced rhyming, the bad spelling (what the fuck is a 'doth'?), the sheer sense of male entitlement – caused me to retch in disgust. In my GCSE Drama practical examination I presented a devised piece in which I defecated onto a copy of Wordsworth's complete works live on stage. It scuppered my chances of becoming Head Girl, but it was definitely worth it.

My higher education was fairly typical. I studied Modern Languages at Oxford University and then stayed on for an MA in Gender Studies where I wrote a groundbreaking dissertation on technopaganism and the corrosive nature of cis-masculine futurity. It's the kind of degree that prepares you for life in the real world.

It was not until university that I composed my first bona fide poetic masterpiece: 'Castrate All White Men'. It was so radical and powerful that the student newspaper refused to publish it. The editor's claim that 'it simply isn't very good' was clearly an excuse to avoid the inevitable controversy that would ensue. I took this rejection as evidence of institutionalised misogyny, and staged a performance-protest by screaming the poem repeatedly in the High Street, smeared in menstrual blood, throwing dead earthworms at passers-by.

Ever since then I have worked tirelessly to produce the most potent and dissident writing ever known to peoplekind. Words can change the world. When queer activists appropriated the word 'gay' from its traditional meaning of 'happy', they achieved their goal of simultaneously increasing gayness and decreasing happiness. Such is the power of language.

I don't write poems; I write eviscerating daggers of truth.

I am currently residing in one of my London properties, a semi-detached three-bedroom in Kensington. The utility room isn't particularly spacious, but my quotidian struggles are what nourish my genius. I feed on misfortune, digest it, and vomit it back out into the ether as a beautiful kaleidoscopic shower.

I have made it my mission to change the world for the better, to follow in the footsteps of such trailblazing luminaries as Emmeline Pankhurst, Rosa Parks and that guy who played Mr Sulu in *Star Trek*. I adore the word 'woke', because our society is a slumbering beast that has been trapped in its coma for far too long. It needs to be nudged.

That's where I come in. I am that formidable beast-nudger. Read on, and with my guidance you too can realise your inner wokeness.

Fuck the Patriarchy

When a woman reaches orgasm with a man she is only collaborating with the patriarchal system, eroticising her own oppression.

Sheila Jeffreys

I have words of wisdom for all young girls. No matter what you do in life, or how much you achieve, you will always be victims of the patriarchy. Understanding this is the key to your empowerment.

Since the dawn of time, and even long before that, women have struggled under the deadweight of patriarchy. The history of womankind is like a sand beetle attempting to traverse the Serengeti with a horse's bollock upon its back. Yes, women in the West can vote, pursue careers and all the other clichés that males are so fond of parroting. Yet the sad truth is that women in our society today are more oppressed than ever before. It is the *illusion* of freedom that makes our oppression all the more devastating. The fact that so many women think they are enjoying their lives only serves to prove my point.

Women's liberation is a mirage. As soon as it seems within your reach, it vanishes. Never let a man tell you that you are not a victim. A malnourished homeless man sleeping in a gutter is still essentially more privileged than the Queen.

Thankfully, activists such as myself – and the likes of Laura Bates, Emma Watson and Caroline Criado-Perez – are toiling relentlessly to inject some long overdue oestrogen into this dying system. I feel a genuine kinship with these fearless defenders of the downtrodden. For one thing, we have friends in common, mostly through the public-school debating circuit or hockey tournaments back in the day. Also, my godparents used to summer in a Swiss resort often frequented by the Criado-Perez family, so we're practically related.

The struggle can be quite dispiriting, as Laurie Penny has outlined in her book *Bitch Doctrine*: 'I've fought for years, since I was a messed-up schoolgirl myself, for a world in which women could be treated like human beings, and sometimes it seems like nothing's changed.' It's almost as if her work has had no impact.

The word 'woman' comes from the Old English for 'female human', whereas 'man' simply means 'human'. Linguistically speaking, this implies that women are deviants from the norm. In order to rectify this, I sometimes refer to men as 'unwomen', and boys as 'ungirls'. I likewise often refer to straight people as 'ungays', so that they too can understand what it feels like to be othered.

Personally, I have little time for cis males. For me, the ideal man is one who, to borrow the late great feminist Andrea Dworkin's phrase, has been 'beaten to a bloody pulp with a high-heel shoved in his mouth, like an apple in the mouth of a pig'. Dworkin was a genius of the highest calibre who produced some of the most perspicacious feminist writing of the twentieth century and was a key activist in the anti-pornography movement. And she managed to achieve all of this with a total lack of charm and a face like a robber's dog. A true inspiration.

Next time you are in close proximity to a male, observe his behaviour carefully. Everything he does is phallic in nature. He stands tall and *erect*, always attempting to dominate. He *strides* from place to place, thrusting his legs outwards, onwards, like he is yearning for copulation. He *spits* his words out, projecting each syllable as though simulating a violent ejaculation. When it comes to men, every gesture, every word, every thought, is an act of sexual aggression.

Some readers may be thinking to themselves, 'But I know some adorable men, who are respectful, charming, and would never dream of upsetting a woman.' Let me nip this delusion in the bud. *No you don't*. If you believe that any man in your life is a pleasant human being, then this only shows the extent to which you have been deceived.

This goes for your father as well, if you are unfortunate enough to have one. I will freely admit to the existence of my male parent, but I keep my distance. I catch sight of him every now and then, usually at funerals, or while I'm casually flicking through the pages of *Tatler* as Nenita finishes off my laundry. But in all honesty, beyond the provision of DNA and a modest trust fund, I cannot see what purpose my father has served.

Men are trained from birth to disregard the desires of women. Come to think of it, the process is initiated long before that. All males begin their lives within the bodies of their mothers. They are literally inside a woman without her verbal consent. I cannot put this explicitly enough. *The very first thing a male does in his life is to rape his own mother.*

The question of how to exist as a woman in a patriarchal world is one that must occupy any truly woke mind. It presents something of a paradox. I have no doubt whatsoever of my innate superiority over men, and yet I still feel oppressed.

In order to obliterate the patriarchy we all need to work in concert to rid our minds of gendered stereotypes. In August 2018, Ann Millington, chief executive of Kent Fire and Rescue, called for the popular children's television character Fireman Sam to be renamed 'Firefighter Sam' in an effort to encourage greater diversity in the services. Millington's point is indisputable. The *only* reason women don't go into firefighting is because they've had no stop-motion animation role models.

Frankly, if some 'fireman' tried to save me from a burning building, I'd tell him to go fuck himself.

The patriarchy is ancient. Our planet has existed for roughly four and a half billion years, which means that there have been four and a half billion years of male tyranny. What we really need is a system of reparations. The optimal solution would simply be to invert the current social order. Women should be paid twice as much as their male counterparts to make up for the injustices of history.

In addition, I would like to see women occupy all major positions of influence: in the media, the judiciary, the arts and politics. It isn't enough for us to have a female Prime Minister, female First Minister of Scotland and female Head of State. These are just tokenistic appointments intended to give the impression of equality. It's a trick.

Women in power rarely make mistakes. Margaret Thatcher does not count, because she was a woman only in a strictly biological sense.

Think about it. If Tony Blair had been female, we would never have been led into a disastrous illegal war in the Middle East. And, as an added bonus, Cherie would have made a splendid lesbian role model.

When women are valued more than men, then and only then will we have achieved true equality.

The Tyranny of Facts

I think that there's a lot of people more concerned about being precisely, factually and semantically correct than about being morally right.
Alexandria Ocasio-Cortez

All knowledge is fleeting. What's true today won't be true tomorrow. The sharpest minds in the world once believed that our fates were dictated by the stars, that the earth was flat, and that the tides were somehow influenced by the moon.

We may scoff at such superstitions now, but in years to come our descendants will laugh heartily when they consider that we blindly accepted the putative link between morbid obesity and poor health, or the idea that black people can't be born in a white body, or that men can't get pregnant. After all, there is nothing more satisfying to a child than the breastmilk of a loving father.

Take chromosomes, for instance. Has anyone ever actually seen one? If you look in scientific textbooks, the best you'll find are a few fuzzy black and white

17

pictures of what look like pipe cleaners twisted into odd shapes. This is sub-Photoshop bullshit.

I would go so far as to say that all knowledge is a patriarchal construct, because it has been acquired over centuries of male totalitarianism. Every time a man speaks, therefore, he is contributing to a culture of androcentric hegemony. In order to remedy this problem, we need to ensure that women today are speaking more than men. This is why I never stop talking, even when I have absolutely nothing of value to say.

Recently the BBC promoted a smartphone app which would assist women to speak up in meetings. This is a huge step forward. How else could women be expected to take the initiative and make their feelings known? If it really were as straightforward as simply asserting oneself then everyone would be doing it.

The conservative broadcaster Ben Shapiro (whose opinions are always wrong) bases much of what he believes on facts, which just goes to show how useless they are. 'Facts don't care about your feelings,' he is known to say. The opposite is true. Feelings don't care about your facts. This is how social justice works. If you *feel* something to be true, then it *is* true.

For those of you who are sceptical on this point, I would simply ask that you defer to my superior wisdom. I have neither the patience nor the inclination to explain myself in full. Let's just say it has something to do with institutionalised power structures and leave it there.

Facts are routinely deployed in order to spread hate. If, for example, you were to ask so-called 'experts' working for the NHS about their views on childhood obesity, they would say that one in every five children is overweight, and that this can lead to enhanced risk of hypertension, type 2 diabetes and heart disease. This is because, for some inexplicable reason, health professionals in this country are given a free pass to behave like a bunch of fat-phobic browbeaters.

If all children were obese, then no one would ever be bullied for being fat. So if you are serious about combatting fat-shaming, you have a responsibility to overfeed your kids.

And what about the recent campaign by Cancer Research UK, a charity that purports to be raising funds to save lives, but is actually spreading hate facts? On a series of posters across the nation, this group made the astonishing claim that obesity is the second most common cause of cancer after smoking. The implication is clear. If you are fat, you deserve to die.

Telling an obese person to lose weight is like telling a person of colour to bleach their skin. It is *not* OK to erase someone's identity like this.

This isn't charity. It's terrorism.

Comedian and activist Sofie Hagen spoke for all of us when she tweeted Cancer Research UK directly – 'Thanks for making the world shittier, you filthy cunts' – a remark which caused quite a stir on social media.

This was extremely fortunate, because just later that week Hagen announced that her book on the subject of obesity would soon be available to buy.

Consider the England football team: each member a slim, athletic cisgender heterosexual male. Sixty-two per cent of adults in the UK are classified as over-weight or obese; how is it possible that a team that claims to represent the nation does not include one single person of girth (POG)? This kind of discrimination is precisely why the fat acceptance movement is so essential.

Football generally lends itself to bigotry. When the England team qualified for the quarter-finals of the 2018 World Cup by beating Colombia, manager Gareth Southgate called it a 'special night for every Englishman'. Observe his choice of language, specifically that offensive term 'English*man*'. This is linguistic gender-based genocide; a violent erasure of female identity. This is Bosnia all over again.

Then there is the pernicious theory known as 'sexual dimorphism'. Anybody who has ever taken even a rudimentary course in Gender Studies will know that there are literally no biological differences between men and women. Except in the case of trans people, who are born in the wrong body.

Males will often cite pseudo-scientific fields of study such as 'biology', 'medicine' or 'endocrinology' to prove that men are the physically stronger sex, although you'd be hard pushed to find a respectable feminist who takes any of this seriously. As Jill Bowling and

Brian Martin confirmed in their landmark essay 'Science: a Masculine Disorder?', the entire discipline is 'embedded in a set of social, economic and political relations embodied through patriarchy'. They call it a 'science-patriarchy system', which is a roundabout way of saying that men invented science in order to justify grabbing women by the tits.

It can hardly be a coincidence that virtually all of the most famous scientists and doctors throughout history have been male. The names that spring most immediately to mind are Dr Crippen, Dr Jekyll and Dr Harold Shipman. This tells us all we need to know.

Then there's Alfred Nobel, the inventor of dynamite – the first mass-produced lethal explosive – which went on to kill hundreds of thousands of innocent people, including his own brother.

And they gave this guy a fucking peace prize.

The theory of sexual dimorphism is perpetuated in the world of sports, where teams are arbitrarily divided into 'male' and 'female'. It has developed out of a genuine gynophobia. Men are simply too scared to compete on an equal footing with women. Like ISIS fighters, who believe that they will be consigned to Hell if they are killed by a female antagonist, men the world over are petrified of a woman beating them at badminton.

In any case, if it is true that men are superior at sports, why is it that transgender athletes tend to win more medals *after* they transition to female?

21

Let's be very clear about this. Any form of segregation of the sexes, in sports, in schools, in toilet facilities – anywhere at all – is a reprehensible form of gender apartheid.

Except when it comes to mosques, in which case it's empowering.

I, Victim

My soul is crucified on your tumescent shaft.
You are that paper-cut that smiles bleedingly
Upon a backbroken orphan freshly rinsed.
A demented piglet wrapped in a leather quilt,
Roarsquealing into the gash of time.

My cadaver lies uneaten at the gates of your treachery.
Pandora's box heaving over with poisoned bile.
You have dined upon my succulent gusset
Like a ragewanking hobgoblin, belching power.
Or a Chinese assassin with fat hands.

But I am woman.
I rise, like the bewigged toad of probity,
Spitting matriarchal cannonballs into the open groin of
    God.
I shall feed you banjo meat from Satan's buffet.
My revenge is gluten-free.

How to Prod a Shepherd

'Shepherds are feral'
Says Uncle Asbjørn,
Grimacing
In the crepuscular wreath of smoke
That cyclones wistfully from his ancient pipe.

I am seven years old, or thereabouts,
Cross-legged on the rug at my uncle's pockmarked feet,
Listening
And gently massaging the rectum of my pet chinchilla
Because that is the way we do things here.

'Approach them with caution.'
Uncle Asbjørn inhales lungly,
Coughing
As he picks a flea from his favourite toenail
And presses the tiny corpse against his wormish
    lips.

'Shepherds exist only to be prodded,'
He whispers, teasing the air with a swollen tongue,
Imagining
His better days as a priapic young shepherd-prodder,
Roaming the fields with a lubricated glove.

The Human Condition

Rabid dreams cut my lips
Screamways into silence
As I tear the spleen from the mulish beekeeper
To spill hurtly onto a blackblue horizon
Like a superstitious louse in a whore's crotch.

A doublepunch to the coleslaw hips,
We reel, dirty sucklove,
Into a yeasty harness of similitude.

You watch me drown
In the blood of my brother's scabrous mind,
And lurking,
Underhand overfoot,
Slice your throat with the frozen piss of Christ.

As a pigeon at the portcullis,
Banged up and bunglefunked,
I give birth to my mother's corpse.

A dryhumped slattern whispers blood,
Reaching into death.
'Somebody forgot to trim the leaves.'
Hagspeak for aeons of binbag sodomy,
Where hollowed-out pygmies prong their spuds into
    silence.

Suck My Hashtag

I was a feminist before it was cool.

Laurie Penny

In early 2018, I decided to become more industrious on social media. I was inspired by other activists who had made use of their online platforms in order to spread their message and explain to people why they are wrong about everything.

In the digital age, the internet is the weapon of choice for anyone who is serious about social justice. The successors to the likes of Martin Luther King and Mahatma Gandhi are now to be found on Twitter, Facebook and Instagram. In many ways these modern-day 'keyboard warriors' have surpassed the work of King, who in any case was on record as saying that he believed people should 'not be judged by the colour of their skin, but by the content of their character'. He clearly knew nothing about intersectionality, and was therefore a self-hating racist.

Thanks to my keen insights and breathtakingly subversive poetry, I rapidly garnered many thousands

27

of followers, or *disciples* as I prefer to call them. But as a woman online, I soon found myself on the receiving end of relentless abuse. I am often accused of being a shrill, humourless tricoteuse. 'Show us on the doll where your father touched you,' said one sarcastic nuisance. The joke's on him, because in actual fact my father used to touch my doll.

Most of the online hatred that comes my way takes the form of criticism of my poetry. 'It doesn't even rhyme,' they say, as though their opinion counts for *anything*. Advice and feedback from a man is about as welcome as an anorectal abscess.

Fuck them all. I douche with white male tears.

In any case, men know nothing about poetry. What male poets have ever amounted to anything? Auden, Coleridge, Poe; overrated subliterate twats, the lot of them. Robert Burns is still lauded as Scotland's national poet in spite of penning such gibberish as: 'We twa hae run about the braes, / And pu'd the gowans fine.' You'd have thought with his degree of success he could afford to hire a proof-reader.

James Joyce is another unjustly glorified male writer. He is credited as being one of the most innovative novelists who ever lived, but could barely construct a coherent sentence. In one of his most famous works, *Finnegans Wake*, he even left the apostrophe out of the title. This is pretty basic stuff.

Social media should be a safe space where I can express myself without fear of being insulted, ridiculed or challenged in any way. All this hatred directed towards me simply proves that my work and activism are more urgent than ever. Nazis may mobilise, but they'll never prevail.

Twitter in particular is a cesspit of the far right. It's got to the point where if someone doesn't have 'anti-fascist' in their bio, it's safest to assume that they're a fascist.

In a sense, one's internet presence is one's true personality. Old-fashioned 'face-to-face' conversation is all very well, but the best way to debate serious political issues is surely through an online forum in which you won't have to deal with the potential intimidation that comes with actual human contact, and thoughts need not be developed beyond a 280-character limit. In addition, it's important to be able to block people who disagree with you to avoid being triggered by challenging opinions.

Social media also leaves an electronic trail, which enables activists like myself to gather evidence to discredit our opponents. For instance, it was recently discovered that James Gunn, director of the *Guardians of the Galaxy* film series, had tweeted some jokes about paedophilia many years ago. In my humble opinion, joking about paedophilia is even worse than actual paedophilia. Don't get me wrong; an act of physical molestation is obviously abhorrent, but at least it can't be retweeted.

Other celebrities who have been rightly shamed by committing violence through online jokes include the comedian and fascist (i.e. Trump supporter) Roseanne Barr, television and radio presenter Maya Jama, Hitler-loving YouTube celebrity PewDiePie, and that odious bespectacled minion of the Antichrist who goes by the name of Toby Young.

Of course, there have been occasions when certain problematic tweets have resurfaced that appear to implicate decent left-wing people. One such example is Sarah Jeong, a brave journalist-cum-activist who works for the *New York Times*. In July 2018 she was promoted to the publication's editorial board, and unfortunately some alt-right trolls had posted some of her old tweets in which she made supposedly offensive jokes about white men.

'Are white people genetically predisposed to burn faster in the sun,' she asked, 'thus logically being only fit to live underground like grovelling goblins?' For all the conservative establishment's talk of thin-skinned 'snowflakes', I find the real snowflakes, like their namesakes, tend to be *white*.

In any case, when Jeong observed that 'it must be so boring to be white' she was merely expressing an uncomfortable truth. Be honest with yourself: have you ever met a white person who isn't bored on some level? White people live conventional lives, they lack imagination, and they can't rap.

I do not fall into this category because I have always felt a profound connection with people of colour. Perhaps it's because when I was growing up most of our staff were Filipinos.

Thankfully, Silicon Valley tech giants have a commendable record of banning users who have problematic opinions, or engage in 'satire'. And it's not as though there has been a lack of transparency. YouTube, Twitter and Facebook have made it explicitly clear which opinions you are allowed to have.

If you don't want to be censored, don't say the wrong things. It really is that simple.

White Death

The dictionary defines racism as 'prejudice, discrimination, or antagonism directed against someone of a different race based on the belief that one's own race is superior'.

The dictionary is wrong.

The true definition of racism is actually an equation. *Racism = prejudice + power*. We know this because left-wing sociologists and activists have made it clear that the people who compiled the dictionary aren't best qualified to explain the meaning of words.

We need to trust the experts. As YouTube personality Franchesca Ramsey puts it: 'If your car breaks down, you don't look up "car" in the dictionary to try and fix it. You go to a mechanic.' And she's absolutely right. Any mechanic worth their salt will tell you that the dictionary definition of 'car' – 'a road vehicle, typically with four wheels, powered by an internal combustion engine and able to carry a small number of people' – is absolute horseshit.

Similarly, the phrase 'white people' is often taken to refer to people who are white. But, as Myriam François-Cerrah has pointed out, 'white people' as a term 'doesn't refer to the colour of people's skin as much as it refers to people's identification with the dominant power relations which continue to subjugate people of colour to a second-class status'.

The sterling work of white feminists such as François-Cerrah has helped us to understand that people of colour (POCs) are invariably persecuted, and that includes those who are wealthy and well-connected. Even Oprah Winfrey is routinely subjected to random searches by police.

I assume this is the case, anyway. I haven't really looked into it.

To be female is difficult enough, but to be black and female is what Frances M. Beal has described as 'double jeopardy'. White women need to get over their misogynoir and accept that there are structural imbalances that secure their privilege. On this matter, I highly recommend Robin DiAngelo's scintillating book *White Fragility*. If you've ever wondered why honkies get so uppity when you call them racist without any apparent justification, this is the book for you.

I use the term 'POC' because it is a convenient way to group all non-whites together without having to go to the trouble of identifying their differences. Needless to say, this is particularly helpful when it comes to oriental countries like Japan, China and Siam, whose citizens are pretty much indistinguishable.

Whiteness *always* equates to structural power, even in predominately black countries. An acquaintance recently tried to suggest to me that, globally speaking, white people are the minority. This is simply absurd. Why would ethnic minorities be called 'ethnic minorities' if they weren't in the minority?

Some people really are fucking idiots.

Besides, whiteness acts as a kind of poison, contaminating all that is laudable in black culture. You may recall the nineties pop band Eternal, who only achieved true artistic success after the white woman left. A single white member of an otherwise black singing group is what is commonly known as a 'spanner in the works'. Louise Redknapp was that spanner, and her inveterate whiteness meant that she couldn't harmonise for shit. 'Just a Step from Heaven' would have been an immortal classic were it not for Redknapp caterwauling in the background like a harpy with a slipped disc.

As activist Rudy Martinez notes, in an article addressed to whites entitled 'Your DNA is an abomination':

White death will mean liberation for all. To you good-hearted liberals, apathetic nihilists, and right-wing extremists: accept this death as the first step toward defining yourself as something other than the oppressor.

Until then, remember this: I hate you because you shouldn't exist.

This cannot be said often enough. It is not racist to hate someone on the basis of their skin colour, *if that person is white*. Indeed, my seething contempt for the Caucasian race is precisely what sustains my art.

The ubiquity of racism is an idea echoed by one of my favourite writers, Afua Hirsch, in her book *Brit(ish): On Race, Identity and Belonging*. Above all, I admire Hirsch's tenacity, because even though she comes from an extremely wealthy family, was privately educated, enjoyed an idyllic childhood complete with 'berry-stained rambles on Wimbledon Common' and 'walking holidays in the Alps', she is still able to see past all that to realise that she is every bit as subjugated as those individuals who were bought and sold during the era of slavery. She is also brave enough to call out the obvious racism of anyone who gave her book a bad review.

Another activist who won't let her wealthy origins detract from her oppression is Munroe Bergdorf, who appeared on BBC One's current affairs show *This Week* in October 2017 to point out that Britain is a 'deeply racist society'. As a person of mixed race, Bergdorf is a true victim. It is not her fault that she inadvertently gives the impression of being an irredeemably pampered cunt.

'The uncomfortable truth,' says Bergdorf, 'is that the white race is the most violent and oppressive force of nature on earth.' The validity of this statement cannot be denied. White people are indisputably privileged, irrespective of their class, economic circumstances, health, age, looks, or whether or not they have all their limbs intact.

Consider, if you will, the example of white American author Helen Keller (1880–1968). Even though she was left deaf and blind following an illness as a baby, she still managed to study for a degree, write twelve books and travel the world to give lectures. This kind of privilege is staggering.

Let us not forget that the history books were written by straight white men, which explains why history as an academic subject is so flagrantly revisionist. How many people, for instance, know or even care that Agatha Christie was a Bangladeshi transwoman?

Earlier this year I decided to spend a month identifying as BAME (Black, Asian and Minority Ethnic), and there's no denying that I experienced some terrible prejudice. You wouldn't believe the looks of disapproval that people gave me when I told them I was an ethnic minority.

In fact, the day after I transitioned to BAME, my personal trainer phoned me up to cancel one of our appointments. This never happened when I was white. I refuse to accept this as mere coincidence.

I'd go so far as to say that being transracial can be even more of an ordeal than being ethnic from birth. It is known as 'wrongskin', and one of the most famous sufferers was the civil rights activist and former president of the National Association for the Advancement of Colored People, Rachel Dolezal. Although born to white parents, Dolezal has always known she was African-American because as a child she would use brown rather than peach crayons to draw pictures of herself. If that isn't the behaviour of a black woman, I don't know what is.

When I was going through my BAME phase I found a similar connection to my ethnic brothers and sisters. I found that my dancing had suddenly improved, I developed a taste for Um Bongo, and I started listening to rap music by the likes of N.W.A. ('Niggaz Wit Acronyms'). It's only since I've retransitioned to white that I've managed to revitalise my love of Enya.

It is no accident that the most effective president in the history of the United States of America has been Barack Obama. Blackness brings with it an innate wisdom. Perhaps it has something to do with ancient tribal forces that are beyond our comprehension. Obama's heart beats in time with the drums of a distant Africa, and his voice rings out in stirring ululations, like the war-cry of a pygmy king echoing through a grass-thatched hut.

I've seen *Black Panther* six times by the way, so I know what I'm talking about.

Many have argued that Obama's legacy is tainted by the fact that on his watch the Democratic Party haemorrhaged support to the Republicans, that he enabled policies of illegal domestic surveillance, doubled the national debt, allowed millions of citizens to fall below the poverty line and was guilty of reckless interventionism in foreign disputes. What these critics forget is that Obama was mixed race, and all of these flaws can be attributed to his white side. If he had been fully black, his legacy would have been irreproachable.

This teaches us that if ever we are to progress towards a woke utopia, white people must atone for, or outright reject, their whiteness. Beware of those who claim that people of colour are capable of being racist, for this is a typical tactic of the far right. Prejudice from one POC to a different kind of POC is known as 'colourism', and is entirely forgivable in the context of their history of disenfranchisement.

In order to sustain the dignity of POCs, we should not be holding them to the same standards as whites.

My Culture Is Not Your Goddam Prom Dress

You can still be homeless and have white privilege.
                                           Munroe Bergdorf

O ne of the ways in which white people wield their structural power is through what's known as *cultural appropriation*. Allow me to illustrate.

In April 2018, a young American student by the name of Keziah tweeted some photographs from her high-school prom. Although Keziah is Caucasian, she had decided to wear a traditional Chinese garment known as a *qipao*. Thankfully, she was called out on social media for her colossal egotism. One Twitter user known as Jeremy Lam, an American man who looks a bit Chinese, responded with 'My culture is NOT your goddam prom dress', helpfully capitalising the word 'not' just in case people read this as an endorsement.

Over forty thousand retweets later, and all of a sudden it was Lam who was at the receiving end of abuse, simply for drawing attention to Keziah's racism. As usual, those who stand up for minorities end up in the firing line. Lam was completely justified in speaking out on behalf of the one billion Chinese people on this planet, who doubtless all felt exactly the same way.

Let me be absolutely clear about where I stand on this issue. Keziah, whoever she is, is a monster. If this white colonialist whorebag had any respect for Chinese culture, she'd have broken her toes and had her feet bound like all proper Chinawomen do.

Cultural appropriation is the principal signifier of white privilege. 'All white people,' states *Guardian* columnist Lola Okolosie, are implicated 'in white supremacy'. In other words, literally every white person you have ever met is a racist. It stands to reason.

Even death cannot save people of colour from the marauding spirit of these white magpies. When Aretha Franklin passed away, a division of guards at Buckingham Palace played a brass band version of 'Respect' and, in doing so, showed that they simply do not comprehend the meaning of the song. Worse still, these white bandsmen appropriated this beautiful black woman's song *on the day of her funeral*. It's gross beyond belief.

It just goes to show how easy it is to fall into the bearpit of racism through mere ignorance. Have you ever used cutlery in Wagamama? Ask yourself why you didn't opt for the chopsticks. The answer is simple: somewhere inside of you, ever so deeply buried, is a venomous racist gremlin.

Sometimes in order to be woke one must make personal sacrifices. For a long while one of my favourite activities was yoga, until I read a dissertation about how the practice had originated in ancient India and was therefore deeply problematic. I was mortified. I had been engaging in an act of cultural genocide simply by sitting in difficult postures on a mat.

I quickly undertook some much needed research, and found a website called 'Decolonizing Yoga', which features a fabulous article by Susanna Barkataki, an Indian woman residing in America who 'often cries on her yoga mat from joy'. I haven't cried since 2004 – and that was only because of conjunctivitis – but I do understand how she feels.

Moreover, I can appreciate her sense of being othered by the white Westerners who so brazenly adopt these oriental practices without taking any time to consider the consequences. It is, as Barkataki points out, a form of colonisation. I would go further and say that for a white person to participate in yoga is effectively to re-enact the British Army's massacre of a thousand Indian civilians at Amritsar in 1919.

'To be colonized is to become a stranger in your own land,' writes Barkataki. 'As a desi, this is the feeling I get in most Westernized yoga spaces today.' Reading this passage stirred acute feelings of guilt within my soul for all the Mountain Poses and Downward Facing Dogs I had performed over the years. As penance, I fasted for a week. Not that I gave up eating as such, but I did refrain from partaking in my favourite dish – smashed avocado salad with grilled kale – which took considerable self-discipline.

More recently, Labour MP Dawn Butler took umbrage at a new brand of 'jerk rice' that had been marketed by television chef Jamie Oliver. 'Your jerk rice is not ok,' Butler tweeted. 'This appropriation from Jamaica needs to stop.' For me, angry tweets addressed to celebrity chefs are what being a Member of Parliament is all about.

Oliver needs to stay in his lane. It is baffling that he felt he could bastardise Caribbean cuisine in a cynical ploy to make money. The very least he could have done is ask permission from Rustie Lee.

Butler, on the other hand, is a hero. It takes considerable courage for a female MP to openly challenge the authority of a male celebrity, particularly one whose every recipe screams toxic masculinity. Let us not forget that white supremacy comes in many forms, and often it can insinuate itself into our culture through microwavable ready-meals.

I am not suggesting that Oliver is evil (he definitely is), but there's a very good chance that he secretly yearns for a white ethno-state. With no evidence to the contrary, this strikes me as the most sensible conclusion. In any case, this was the man who spent years campaigning to eliminate childhood obesity in schools, which is taking fat-shaming to genocidal extremes.

Artists such as myself also need to be keenly aware of the impact of our choices on marginalised groups. When white writers put words into the mouths of black characters it is known in the literary sphere as 'crackerblack'. We're all familiar with the concept. Some of the more cringeworthy examples of crackerblack can be found in the films of Quentin Tarantino or the more offensive novels of Mark Twain. Most famous of all is the play *Othello*, in which our supposed 'great bard' tried his hand at a kind of Moorish patois. 'I kissed thee ere I killed thee: no way but this, killing myself, to die upon a kiss.' Find me one black man who speaks like that.

The more that white writers insist on straying into black culture, the more I'm convinced that burning books and works of art is occasionally the right thing to do. When I've said this in the past, I have been accused of perpetuating a similar ideology to that of ISIS who, as we all know, have destroyed historical artefacts in Iraq, Syria and Libya. Needless to say, I am no supporter of ISIS. I simply believe that problematic art needs to be expunged in order to preserve a free and civilised society.

And say what you will about ISIS, but at least they're not Islamophobic.

Cultural Appropriation

Thief of culture.
You slither hamstyle with dreadlocked hands,
Clenching in a calypso chokehold of bindi banditry,
Moistened by an ego semi-fried in foreign oils,
Withdrawing into striptease fissures of night.
You will never be Aswad.

Plunderbeast of history.
My ancestors scream in your hollow wigwam,
Ghostrolling in the ectoplasm of your hate.
I staunch the flow of simpering tribal sauce,
A digital sombrero clings deafblind
To a face falsely smeared in a coalish hue.

Filcher of rice.
Parades at promtime in a fraudulent frock,
A gurning juggernaut of stunted envy,
Appropriating my soul, my gaylord shoes.
The death-minstrel who leaps backwards onwardly,
Washing away the past with your piss of lies.

The Scourge of Whiteness

Whiteness is a chattering virus,
Bare-chested and brutal,
Gilded and gelded,
Bearing beer-stained flags that skitter
In the rattling zephyr of Farage's death-sneeze.

Citizens half-Hitlered,
Fattened on reveries of Brexit
And laminated honky llama cream.
Herds that coalesce into a giant colonial lozenge,
Throttling their foes with septic bunting.

Memories of a future with invisible swastikas
Tattooed onto lager-stuffed livers.
Angry male feet attack synthetic spheres of leather,
Strike them into nets like migrant heads.
Anglo-chat speakly for the hopscotch juice.

Whiteness is rape,
A terrifying blancmange of spite
In a landscape laden with severed hands applauding.
Crabwise, it dances on the fudge of eternity
And gets twatted on the breath of a half-fisted pig.

My Angry Vagina

My growler growls.
Plucked-up and back-eared
It chewmunches through
Patriarchal savannahs,

Slipping into packs of males with a toothful grin
To tug and wreck with lady cave precision
Centuries of bap-slapping tyranny
And overtures of porksworded sicklust.

So to the foe I skiphopjump,
Biting man-skin with deadly spreadlegs,
My ravenous clunge grazes on their grazes.
Vagina dentata.

Beyond a bent matrix of doom I soar:
Sucked up, fucked up, fluently wombed,
Frigging my way to an openclosed eye socket,
My snatch screams for justice.

Why I'm No Longer Talking to Men About Feminism

To call a man an animal is to flatter him; he's a machine, a walking dildo.

Valerie Solanas

Ours is a loud, crass, male world. I mean that literally. The planet we live on is the shape of a testicle, for fuck's sake.

It should come as no surprise, therefore, that virtually all of my female associates are activists. One of my most radical friends is Cassandra (the second 's' is silent) who is passionate about poststructuralist gender theory and vegan bloodsports. She recently produced her own series of online vlogs in order to raise awareness about toxic masculinity in the amateur hemp-weaving community. It wasn't as successful as she'd hoped, partly because nobody seemed to be interested.

Last week she overheard some construction workers talking about Jodie Whittaker, the actor who made history when she was cast as the first ever female

Doctor Who. According to Cassandra, these men were discussing how attractive they found Whittaker, and there was even some coarse remark about her breasts. It goes without saying that women shouldn't have to put up with this kind of filth when they are innocently eavesdropping on other people's conversations.

But this is about so much more than a timelord's mammary glands. There can be few examples of misogyny more virulent than a man finding a woman attractive. Worse still, such sexual objectification is very difficult to police, because often these thoughts remain unarticulated. Sometimes, men pleasure themselves when they are alone and think about the women they know.

Just take a moment to consider the implications of this. It could be you. It could be your daughter. He could be fantasising about an incestuous orgy in which he penetrates your grandmother while she, in turn, is busy stimulating the clitorises of two of your favourite aunts. Every time you speak to a man I would like you to remember this, and the likelihood that even during the course of your polite conversation this image is simmering away in his depraved brain.

Personally, I would rather be boiled alive in a giant crucible of yak's piss than have a man look at me without my consent.

In spite of our efforts, fourth-wave feminism has yet to eradicate male sexuality in its entirety. We successfully campaigned to ban the topless models on Page 3 of the *Sun* newspaper, and yet men in this country are still lusting after women. I find it baffling. If I didn't know better, I'd assume there was something instinctive about it.

But thanks to the #MeToo movement, more men than ever have been called out for their sexual misconduct. The right-wing commentariat has, inevitably, argued that we have created a culture in which due process has been reversed, and men are presumed guilty from the outset.

Good.

I believe all women. All of them. Under all circumstances.

Let's take the example of Roxanne Pallett, an actor who appeared in the 2018 television series *Celebrity Big Brother*, in which a group of well-loved public figures, along with the psychic Sally Morgan, resided together for two weeks in full view of the cameras. Controversy ensued when Pallett claimed that fellow actor Ryan Thomas had repeatedly punched her. Many were sceptical.

I believed Roxanne. I still believe Roxanne. Even when footage was released which made it clear that there was barely any physical contact, I still believed Roxanne. Even when she apologised for lying, I still believed Roxanne. Video evidence has got fuck all to do with her lived experience.

As feminists, we have a responsibility to believe women. The stakes are too high. If Roxanne is not to be believed, other women who haven't been punched might not have the courage to come forward.

In any case, no man is innocent. Even though Thomas didn't hit her in a physical sense, you can be sure he has transgressed in other ways during his lifetime. I think feminist filmmaker Emily Lindin put it best when she said, 'I'm actually not at all concerned about innocent men losing their jobs over false sexual assault harassment allegations. If some innocent men's reputations have to take a hit in the process of undoing the patriarchy, that is a price I am absolutely willing to pay.'

Lindin should be congratulated. Few individuals would be brave enough to see other people's lives ruined for the sake of a greater cause.

Brett Kavanaugh, the Supreme Court justice whose nomination procedure was dogged by allegations of sexual assault, is a further case in point. I was very impressed with the novelist Stephen King, who during the hearing simply tweeted 'I believe the woman.' I'm assuming, of course, that this was in reference to the accusations against Kavanaugh, because if it was a review of *To Kill a Mockingbird* then frankly it's in very poor taste.

There is nothing natural about male sexuality. I remember distinctly when I was a very young girl my grandfather used to hug me. Thanks to an article by Rebecca Leys on the *Everyday Feminism* website – '9 Intersectional Parenting Tips for Parents with Privilege' – I now realise what a predatory old creep he really was.

Leys stresses the importance of 'informed consent' when it comes to raising children. There should be 'no hugs for relatives, no sitting on Santa's lap, no kisses for mummy unless they understand what is being asked of them and they want to do it'. I am prepared to concede that this might be a tad overprotective. Sitting on Santa's lap is fairly harmless on the whole, so long as in advance a parent or guardian checks thoroughly that Santa hasn't got an erection.

Boys are taught to lust after women early in life, mostly through video games and demeaning images in advertising, such as the scantily clad women on the Protein World posters, or that slut rabbit who used to sell Cadbury's Caramel.

Children's television is similarly insidious. The Smurfs may have been people of colour, but theirs was an unforgivably male culture. When the first female Smurf was introduced into the series, she was given the debasing name of 'Smurfette', as though her entire identity was based on the negation of manhood. Likewise, He-Man in the *Masters of the Universe* cartoons, with his rippling muscles and phallic sword, reeked of toxic masculinity.

On the plus side, He-Man was at least progressive enough to announce his pronouns.

Part of the problem is that men won't even attempt to address their own misogyny. Writer and activist Talia Lavin has shown how 'most men view women as members of a separate, inscrutable & ultimately inferior species, even if they would never say so'. For the majority, women are 'beyond the barrier of empathetic imagination'. What I *love* about Lavin is not only that she's a fierce feminist, but that she can read the minds of *all men*. She's like a cross between Lena Dunham and The Amazing Kreskin.

And it isn't wholly a matter of lasciviousness. Males are intrinsically aggressive creatures; in any difficult situation, their first instinct is to resort to violence. How many times have you seen a man kick a garden gnome in frustration, or throw boulders at a passing owl? Ninety-five per cent of prisoners in the UK are male, and of those one hundred percent have criminal records. The implications of these statistics should require no further elucidation.

Even those males who resist their base compulsions and manage to stay within the law are merely thugs in waiting. Recently I was travelling on the Underground in London, because Daddy's driver was off work with gout, and I happened to see a woman struggling on the stairs with a large suitcase. A man in his early thirties stopped and asked whether she would like some assistance.

Naturally, I stepped right in there and called him out for his disgusting sexism. Imagine being so entitled, I told him, to think that women need help in order to lift heavy items. He was genuinely shocked, which plainly reveals how accustomed he must have been to getting his own way. This patriarchal technique used to be known as 'chivalry', but it's really a means by which men can further prove their dominance.

As I watched that woman straining to lift her suitcase, I felt an overwhelming sense of pride that I had saved her from the indignity of succumbing to male arrogance. I would have helped her myself, but I had a train to catch.

The essence of toxic masculinity, then, is the preservation of a phallocentric hierarchy. And this can be enacted through violence, rape or the passive-aggressive carrying of luggage.

Ecosexuality

I'd quite happily fuck a hedge.

St Francis of Assisi

We all know how romantic entanglements with males can go. One minute he's inviting you into his home for an innocent cup of coffee, the next you're at the bottom of a well in his basement applying copious quantities of lotion.

Men are predators. This is the nature of toxic masculinity. As Laurie Penny puts it, 'nice guys rape, and they do it often'. Some of the nicest men I've ever known have been serial rapists.

Heterosexuality, in any case, is a seriously repugnant lifestyle choice. No woman should accept the tyranny of male attention. Some radical feminists such as Sheila Jeffreys have long advocated 'political lesbianism', which suggests that even those women who find men attractive should eschew them in favour of their own sex. It's a concept I explored in my poem 'Haphazard Death Minge', which was published on my friend's online blog *Yonic Reverberations*. Do check it out: it's mostly a combination of feminist crosswords and various black and white stills of Carol Decker.

From my perspective, political lesbianism was never really an option. For one thing I could never get the hang of billiards, which I'm told is a lesbian sport. Nor was I much cop at cunnilingus, possibly due to my mild claustrophobia. Apart from my love of poetry there is very little about me that qualifies as sapphic.

Which brings me on to ecosexuality. Some have accused me of indulging in a fad, but in actual fact I have always found plantlife to be inherently erotic. As a young teenager I would feel an inexplicable frisson whenever I passed through a garden centre. The Japanese anemones I considered particularly sensual, and I would often tickle their stamens when nobody was looking.

Ecosexuality is not a choice, but if it were it would be a choice that I would freely make. Plants are so much more accommodating than men. I am currently in a very fulfilling relationship with a cactus called Josh. The sex is difficult, but not impossible. That's what tweezers were invented for.

And it's not just about carnal fulfilment. Our relationship is far more cerebral than anything I have ever experienced with the opposite sex. The mucilage that Josh secretes from time to time is far smarter than the average male.

People claim that ecosexuality is merely an indulgence of bourgeois leftists who have become obsessed with the politics of identity. In fact, ecosexuality has a long history, dating back to early 2017.

It was pioneered by former porn star turned sex educator Annie Sprinkle and art professor Beth Stephens. These visionary women have rejected the concept of Nature as a mother, and see her instead as a lover. As Stephens says, 'in a misogynistic society, when people imagine the Earth as a "she", they think she is less important than a he. So, the mostly all-male polluting corporate heads think they can treat the Earth badly.' Climate change, in other words, has only come about because men see the earth as a woman, and wish to punish her for being such an uppity wench.

But sex can also be a form of activism. This is why it is imperative that we reject male sexual attention. The penis is a phallic symbol. As such, when women choose to commit sexual intercourse with a male, they are literally allowing themselves to be fucked by the patriarchy. Conventional sex is an act of violence. But there is nothing more sublime than the sight of a Marxist cultural critic shoving chrysanthemums into her twat.

Let us not forget that plants are essentially more progressive than human beings. Many flowers, for instance, are bisexual, with both stamens and ovaries. That the LBGTQIA+ community hasn't yet fully accepted its floral allies is a travesty.

I lost my virginity to a bonsai tree; quite by accident, I'll admit, but that hardly matters. Ever since then I have understood the need to embrace Nature in all her glorious voluptuousness. Those who dismiss ecosexual urges as a perversion of the modern left are typically the kind of unreconstructed bigots who believe that there are only two genders, or that Islam is not a race.

Although utterly marginalised in popular culture, there are signs that ecosexuality is likely to infiltrate the mainstream in the not-too-distant future. In Japan, hentai pornography often includes depictions of women being penetrated by tendrils, and in most cases they seem genuinely to enjoy it. There are rumours that a new Hollywood adaptation of John Wyndham's novel *The Day of the Triffids* is currently in production, but with a radical alteration to the plot; instead of murdering the earth's inhabitants, the alien plants invest in second-hand Ford Escorts for the purposes of dogging.

In addition, applications to botany courses at universities are at an all-time high, doubtless owing to the erotic appeal of the curriculum. Kew Gardens in London has seen steadily increasing attendance figures over the past decade, with many visitors showing signs of overt sexual arousal; acts of frottage are not uncommon in the arboretum. Better still, topiary is becoming more explicitly sexual, with many shrubs in public parks being refashioned into suggestive shapes.

Ecosexual celebrities are becoming more and more vocal. MSNBC host Rachel Maddow has recently announced her intention to become the first woman to be impregnated by a western skunk cabbage. The physiological details have yet to be ironed out, but her publicist is liaising with geneticists to see what can realistically be achieved.

Many of my readers will be sceptical, but take a moment to think about it. Virtually all of us at some point in our lives will have dabbled in bestiality, whether that be a long-term monogamous relationship with a favourite whippet or simply the occasional digit drunkenly inserted into a vole on a night out.

Why, then, is this kind of sexual experimentation considered socially acceptable, when a fling with a climbing hydrangea would be universally condemned?

Ecosexuality is essential for all those who are motivated by social justice, because without it we are merely perpetuating the vile hypocrisy that underpins the conventional sexual mores dictated by our patriarchal overlords.

Find a plant and fuck it. It's not so much a choice as a duty.

Brexit and the Rise of
the Fourth Reich

*I fear Brexit could be the beginning of the destruction
of not only the EU but also Western political civilisation in its entirety.*
Donald Tusk, President of the European Council

We are living through a dangerous period in British history. Acid attacks, knife crime, female genital mutilation, grooming gangs, terrorism; all of these things are now commonplace thanks to the referendum that resulted in a decision to leave the European Union.

The EU is a wonderful thing. It seeks to promote a socialist utopia by masquerading as an exponent of aggressively pro-corporate neoliberalism. It might *appear* to be a horribly right-wing bureaucratic protectionist bloc that prioritises a ruthlessly capitalistic worldview, but this is part of its genius. That's why any socialist worth her salt will have voted Remain. If Che Guevara, Leon Trotsky and Jesus Christ could have got their heads together to invent the ideal political system to promote their values, the EU would have been the outcome.

If anyone is still in any doubt that the far right is enjoying a resurgence, then Brexit should have settled that question once and for all. It never ceases to amaze me how defensive Brexit voters get when you point out that they're fascists. The question on the ballot paper may as well have been 'Do you hate foreigners?'

To borrow the words of Eddie Izzard, this 'hate-fuelled' and 'vicious' Brexit was caused by 'the whining right'. As an ageing cross-dressing professional clown, there can be no one better qualified than Izzard to teach us about the intricacies of international politics.

As Izzard observes: 'Winston Churchill had a dream of a Europe of united countries. He had to fight the extreme right to try and make it happen back in the 1940s, as we have to fight them now to try and make it happen again.' I've been told that there was also a well-known politician called Sir Oswald Mosley who urged us to create a United States of Europe. I must confess I hadn't heard of him before, but he sounds like the kind of visionary we need right now.

If nothing else, this entire mess has prompted a new debate about the validity of democracy, which only works if people vote the right way. The year 2018 saw the centenary of the suffragettes' successful campaign to win the vote for those groups who had been previously disenfranchised: women and working-class men. It turns out they got it half-right. It was the working classes that tipped the scales in favour of leaving the EU. Hindsight is a brutal governess.

The referendum result was baffling for many reasons, not least because the electorate were explicitly *told* how they were meant to vote and still managed to fuck it up. There's really no helping some people.

The UK government had even gone to the trouble of spending ten million pounds of taxpayers' money on leaflets, dispatched to every household in the country, explaining exactly why we needed to stay in the EU. Afterwards, a lot of people were angry about the inclusion of the words: 'This is your decision. The government will implement what you decide.' Admittedly, the phrasing was clumsy. What they actually meant to write was: 'This vote is advisory. The government will ignore your advice.' This isn't the first time that typographical errors have caused confusion.

Democracy is not, and has never been, about accepting the will of the majority. As Winston Churchill put it, 'The best argument against democracy is a five-minute conversation with the average voter.' Or, as Labour MP David Lammy said, 'the government's "will of the people" mantra is bollocks'.

But there may be a solution to this mess. I've recently discovered that the population of Syria is roughly the same as the number of people who voted for Brexit. Why don't we simply do a swap? This would not only eliminate racism in Britain overnight, but by relocating the entire population of Syria to the UK it would also mean that those millions of people would no longer have to live in a country ravaged by civil war.

By the time this book is published, I am confident that there will have been a second referendum. After all, only 1,269,501 more people voted to Leave than to Remain. No serious mathematician would consider that any kind of 'majority'.

Of course, we can't be sure that a second vote would go our way, so really we'd better start campaigning for a third referendum right now. We need to be one step ahead of these scheming Brexiteers.

The movement for a second referendum has received unprecedented support from a number of beloved public figures, including Tracey Ullman, Deborah Meaden, Gabby Logan, John Oliver and Sir Patrick Stewart. One of the unwritten rules of a democracy is that referendums can be overturned if a sufficient number of rich celebrities demand it.

Sting, Bob Geldof and Björn Ulvaeus from ABBA have also stated their opposition to Brexit. Still no word from Sinitta or Duran Duran. Their silence is deafening.

The most influential proponent for a 'People's Vote' is, of course, the ex-footballer Gary Lineker. As one Twitter activist put it, 'Brexiteers are terrified of Linekar [*sic*] because he's got broad appeal.' It is undeniable that Lineker always inspired terror. That's what made him so perfect for advertising crisps.

In any case, the first result was invalid. The number of people who participated in the referendum was

33,551,983. If we break down the support for Leave by demographic, there are some interesting findings: 36.7 per cent of the voters are elderly, and will be dead fairly soon; 49.9 per cent were below average intelligence; 29.1 per cent were what *Guardian* columnists have described as 'low-information' (also known as 'working-class'); and 14.5 per cent had gone into the polling booth by accident and just ticked a box to avoid embarrassment. When all of this is taken into account, it would seem that only 2.4 per cent of the population legitimately voted Leave, which to my mind nullifies the entire process.

People are far too sentimental about the elderly. I am no longer helping them to cross the street. They opted for Brexit, so as far as I'm concerned they can take their chances with the traffic. Remember, too, that these are the people who fought in the Second World War. How can shooting at Germans be anything other than xenophobic?

For my part, I have decided to thwart Brexit through a trilogy of poems (reproduced on the following pages). One is called 'A Little Boy's Brexit', a powerful and poignant piece that beautifully expresses the horrors of leaving the EU from the perspective of a nine-year-old child. Feel free to photocopy the poem and send it to your local MP.

As a further gesture of defiance, I recently changed my pet cat's name to 'Stop Brexit' and, when the vet called for her in the waiting room, all the other animals applauded.

A Little Boy's Brexit

Why are we leaving Europe, Mummy?
Mrs Wilson says I'm doing really well at my French
    lessons,
And Maisie wants to learn Irish dancing,
And we all love to eat pizza on Friday nights.
Why does Theresa May hate us so much?

Why are we leaving Europe, Mummy?
Is it because our bananas aren't bendy enough?
Is it because of that nasty old Mr Farage?
Is it because of Dr Patel who took my tonsils out?
Or is it because those fishermen had a row with Bob
    Geldof?

Why are we leaving Europe, Mummy?
Daddy says everybody will lose their jobs,
And hospitals and schools will shut down,
And mummies and daddies will start eating their own
    babies,
And I'll have to go back on the game again.

Why are we leaving Europe, Mummy?
It seems like such a lovely place,
With all those cute old buildings and pointy towers
And mountains and rivers and sunny beaches
And access to a single market with lucrative free-trade
    arrangements.

23 June 2016

Recoiling from the continent unmoored,
This ark of xenophobic firing squads,
As cattled clowns are tossed off overboard
Beyond an empire's grave of foamy clods.
Emerging from the prick of Churchill's ghost,
Abandoned spectres trussed by their mistrust
And bluepassported gremlins coast to coast.
A widowed nation lured by lemming-lust,
Deceived and semi-felched we blindly plunge
To racist bubblebaths of broken dreams.
A kingdom drowned and dropkicked in the clunge,
Democracy now stuffed with hateful schemes.
Our hopes are flailing, hurtled in the air
Abruptly from the cliffs of Fuckknowswhere.

Brexit: A Haiku

Fuck fuck fuck fuck fuck
Fuck fuck fuck fuck fuck fuck fuck
Fuck fuck fuck fuck fuck.

Pussy Power

I was a lady, not like that cunt Bette Davis.

Joan Crawford

As a sororal collective, feminists have worked hard to let women know that they should be able to live their lives however they please, so long as their decisions are empowering. For any women who are in doubt, reading books by activists such as myself will enable them to make the correct choices and achieve true independence.

This is most important when it comes to one's career. Every single woman has a moral obligation to step up and do their bit to redress the imbalance that we see in so many areas of the job market. In the USA, women make up 97.7 per cent of preschool and kindergarten teachers but only 1.1 per cent of mining machine operators. We need to rectify such appalling inequality through more effective socialisation. Let's start by throwing our daughters into pits with pneumatic drills from time to time.

A real woman is one who is able to turn her oppression to her own advantage, and who does not deviate from the proscribed feminist ideals. We were all horrified to learn that 53 per cent of American women had voted for Donald Trump. This statistic inevitably leads us to ask how they could be so complicit in elevating this self-confessed 'pussy-grabber' to the White House. But, as Suzanne Moore explained in the *Guardian*, 'misogyny is not a male-only attribute'. After all, which is more likely: that there are millions of women who do not share Moore's political opinions, or that there are millions of women who hate themselves? I think the answer is obvious.

Internalised misogyny is out of control. If you're not a feminist, you're not really a woman. Intersectional trailblazer Linda Sarsour caused some controversy when she said of conservative writer Brigitte Gabriel and activist Ayaan Hirsi Ali: 'I wish I could take their vaginas away – they don't deserve to be women.' When her statement was challenged by a Dartmouth College student during one of her lectures, Sarsour simply refused to answer on the grounds that he was a 'white man'. That's the wonderful thing about identity politics; you never have to explain yourself, or even develop your thoughts into what right-wingers call a 'coherent argument'.

For the sake of expedience, I would like you to remember this simple rule of thumb:

> *Men who disagree with feminists = misogynists*
>
> *Women who disagree with feminists = internalised misogynists*

In either case they are to be ignored, not debated.

Some of these self-hating women have become frighteningly influential. I am thinking in particular of Christina Hoff Sommers, Camille Paglia and Ella Whelan, a trio of gorgons of the most oleaginous kind who should never, in any civilised society, be offered a platform to air their dangerous views. Here are some examples:

Women are not children. We are not fragile little birds who can't cope with jokes, works of art, or controversial speakers. Trigger warnings and safe spaces are an infantilizing setback for feminism – and for women.

Christina Hoff Sommers

The problem with too much current feminism, in my opinion, is that even when it strikes progressive poses, it emanates from an entitled, upper-middle-class point of view. It demands the intrusion and protection of paternalistic authority figures to project a hypothetical utopia that will be magically free from offense and hurt.

Camille Paglia

Perpetually portraying women as weak and vulnerable, at every turn, contemporary feminism undermines women's autonomy.

Ella Whelan

What a bunch of hateful bitches.

All three of these internalised misogynists have openly disputed the idea of the gender pay gap. It is a scandal that women in the UK are paid 76p for every £1 a man earns, even though pay discrimination between the sexes has been illegal since 1970. Ryanair, for instance, has a gender pay gap of 72 per cent. How are the CEOs not behind bars?

The company has tried to weasel its way out of its responsibilities by pointing out that most of their pilots are male and most of their cabin crew are female. But the question one must ask is: why are the pilots paid more than the people who serve the drinks? I've seen *Top Gun*. Flying a plane looks like a piece of piss compared to carting around a tray of pork scratchings and mini bottles of gin for the benefit of ungrateful package-holiday gyppos.

If it really was the case that women could simply work towards the necessary qualifications to apply for the better-paid jobs, there'd be no reason to prevent them from doing so. Personally, I wouldn't even bother applying for a course in aviation because I know that some paunchy male executive would probably just spunk onto my curriculum vitae and throw it in the bin.

Recently the BBC were caught paying their US news editor Jon Sopel considerably more than their China news editor Carrie Gracie, simply on the grounds that stories relating to the USA are far more frequently reported. It's sickening to know that our beloved national broadcaster would pay a woman less money for less work.

And in the entertainment industry the disparity is even more extreme. Tom Cruise's estimated net worth is somewhere in the region of 550 million dollars. Su Pollard, on the other hand, is worth a measly 2 million. It should go without saying that male and female actors should be paid equally.

The day my intersectional feminist poetry earns me as much as a male banker is the day the gender pay gap can be declared a myth.

Wedlocked

Marriage is a patriarchal oubliette of doom; a heterosexist institution that has been incarcerating women for centuries. The word 'marriage' comes from the Old French '*marier*', which means 'to marry', so there's no getting around its meaning.

The philosophical principle behind marriage is, quite simply, the commodification of women. We are yoked like bulls at a market and sold off as chattel. There is no such thing as a happily married woman, only those who are suffering from an acute form of Stockholm Syndrome.

The sight of a couple at a wedding – him in a black suit, her in the obligatory billowing white taffeta garb of slavery – is one of the most violent images that could possibly be conjured. It connotes the height of heteronormativity, that invisible matrix of oppression that has enmeshed the globe from the very beginning

81

of civilisation. Until marriage is abolished we shall be less than beasts. There is a very good reason why you will never see a married cat.

But why do women do it? I share Laurie Penny's view that women should 'reject marriage and partnership en masse', and I sincerely hope that the dozen or so people who've read her book will start spreading this important message.

It all comes down to education. Most girls are taught from an early age that their ultimate destiny is to find a 'prince' or a 'knight in shining armour'. The fairy tales are full of it. Disney films, for instance, invariably pair off the pretty female lead with a broad-chested hero with a chiselled profile and searing blue eyes. Take, for instance, Disney's version of *The Hunchback of Notre Dame*, in which the young gypsy girl Esmerelda eventually marries Captain Phoebus. Personally, I'd rather fuck the hunchback.

This damsel-in-distress narrative is bolstered every time a member of the royal family decides to get hitched, which inevitably sparks the kind of drawn-out spectacle of unctuous nationwide fawning that really boils my menses. When Prince William got married, the British citizens were granted a public holiday. Let them eat cake, indeed.

As a form of protest, I spent the entire day working on a new poem, taking breaks only to spit at the news coverage on the television screen. The one thing that made the day bearable was the gratifying sight of streaks of phlegm dribbling down the smug digitised face of Nicholas Witchell.

In any case, as an intersectional social justice activist the very core of my being is rooted in the tenet of anti-monarchism. The fact that Prince George has yet to come out as non-binary tells us all we need to know about the bigotry inherent in the royal family.

And the less said about Meghan Markle the better; the self-identified feminist who nonetheless degraded herself by marrying that bumptious, decadent, champagne-swilling, swastika-clad, ginger runt.

Incidentally, I have nothing against gingers. They should of course be treated in exactly the same way as normal people. But Prince Harry is just the latest manifestation of a corrupt and outmoded class system. I should know. I met him at one of Daddy's soirées in Capri.

Markle is an opportunistic witch. Marrying a prince is just about the least feminist thing you can do. If she was genuinely committed to the cause of female emancipation, she'd throw herself under a horse or something.

Besides, the so-called 'special day' is a humiliating affair. Most traditional ceremonies are presided over by a priest; a male so supercilious that he declares to be channelling the power of an omniscient being. If that wasn't debasing enough, the ritual commences with the priest checking to see if the bride's hymen is intact. If she fails this test, she is declared a whore and the congregation are invited to tear the dress from her sullied body to repeated cries of 'shame'.

I should admit that I've never actually been to a wedding, but I've got no reason to assume that this isn't how it works.

Some women are tricked into the state of housewifery by a delusion known commonly as 'love'. But there is no such thing as love. It is a bourgeois invention intended to justify the psychosexual urges of males.

The most famous 'love story' of all time is about a paedophile called Romeo who successfully seduces a thirteen-year-old child called Juliet. Modern adaptations tend to cast older actors to play Juliet in order to disguise the inherent perversion that the play seeks to normalise. When I was at university, I cast my little sister Sophie in the role of Juliet against a burly Romeo in his late fifties. Sophie was three years old at the time. She couldn't deliver the lines particularly well, but at least the truly depraved nature of the text came across loud and clear.

But what really sets my teeth on edge is that many believe this playwright to be one of the most influential literary figures of all time. He wasn't. He was a knob.

Of course there are financial advantages to marriage, particularly in the case of a lesbian wedding where there are two dowries. But tax benefits and gifts are no compensation for a lifetime of subjugation. The notion of becoming 'one flesh' with a male is a form of corporeal pollution. In order to preserve one's female power, one must reject any kind of connubial vassalage.

I should point out that I write this in the knowledge that my sister is soon to be married and that she intends to ask me to be her 'Maid of Honour'.

I'll do it. But I'll be free bleeding in a white dress.

Towards an Intersectional Socialist Utopia

The move from a structuralist account in which capital is understood to structure social relations in relatively homologous ways to a view of hegemony in which power relations are subject to repetition, convergence, and rearticulation brought the question of temporality into the thinking of structure, and marked a shift from a form of Althusserian theory that takes structural totalities as theoretical objects to one in which the insights into the contingent possibility of structure inaugurate a renewed conception of hegemony as bound up with the contingent sites and strategies of the rearticulation of power.

Judith Butler

Although class has never been one of my priorities as an activist, I do understand what it feels like to endure economic hardship. I'm still making payments on my second wine fridge. And I know plenty of working-class people. Kate Middleton, for instance.

My parents have always voted Tory. Mummy has to really; she's one of the party's key benefactors, so it might send mixed signals if she suddenly decided to support Labour. In spite of this, I've ended up as a steadfast socialist, which just goes to show what a nonconformist free-thinker I am.

Also, it really pisses off my parents, which is hugely satisfying.

It is ironic that the only two female prime ministers in the history of British politics have hailed from the Tory party, given that the laissez-faire economic system is traditionally favoured by males. Capitalism, after all, is a singularly male phenomenon. The ultimate symbol of capitalism, the skyscraper, is nothing more than a giant cock on the horizon, fucking the heavens.

It is no exaggeration to say that I would rather be living in a Soviet gulag than a capitalist country.

Socialism is the principle that everyone deserves to be equal, even the poor. Critics point to the fact that socialist governments in the past have failed to eliminate poverty. But this is a misunderstanding of our aims. If there were no poor people, then there would be no point in socialism, which would make us all capitalists by default. And why would anyone want that?

That conceded, it is the duty of all stalwart socialists to do everything in our power to give succour to the destitute. Only the other day a homeless girl asked me for change. Instead of giving her money, I performed some improvised slam poetry about the evils of economic inequality.

She was literally speechless.

On the whole, class is something of a distraction from the real issues. If the social justice movement has taught us anything, it's that sexuality, gender and race are far more likely to affect your potential for social mobility than economic circumstances, education or nepotism. This is why it was so important for Barack Obama to become president of the United States, because even though the lives of poor black people didn't improve during his tenure, they could at least console themselves with the fact that, for eight years at least, there wasn't some dumbass cracker in the Oval Office.

For me, any political outlook that fails to engage with intersectionality is ideologically moribund. Identity politics has never been a great vote-winner, but there's more to running a country than having the support of the populace.

Just look at Hillary Clinton. Close analysis of the election results shows that she would have become president had she won a lot more votes. But this would have entailed broadening her appeal to those who aren't interested in social justice. In fact, so determined was she to put off potential voters, she referred to Trump supporters as 'deplorables'. If any of them were wavering, she certainly didn't wish to be tainted with their endorsement at the ballot box.

Clinton's plan worked beautifully. She lost the election and thereby retained the moral high ground.

You can't be woke unless you embrace intersectionality. It's a long word, so some of you might find it difficult to comprehend at first, particularly if you were educated in a state school. Or if you're Welsh.

Let me explain. Intersectionality works like a net, with marginalised groups crosshatching at various junctures on the matrices of persecution. Think of it as a hierarchy. So, for instance, a woman is an oppressed figure because we live in a patriarchy, but not so oppressed as a Hispanic woman, who in turn is not so oppressed as a Hispanic lesbian, who in turn is not so oppressed as a Hispanic translesbian with shingles, and so on.

Consider the 2017 'Women's March'. Across the globe hordes of angry activists joined forces to protest about a great many things – nobody was quite sure what in particular – but all of the various groups in attendance were united by their desire to rebuke the millions of citizens who had voted for the wrong candidate in the US election. For a misogynist such as Donald Trump, the sight of scores of women wearing pink 'pussy-hats' – many attired in full-body vagina costumes – must have been terrifying. I'm genuinely surprised that he didn't resign then and there. I'm assuming he didn't hear Ashley Judd reading that epic 'Nasty Woman' poem, because if he had it would have been the end of his presidency for sure.

As far as I'm concerned, you're not entitled to call yourself a feminist if you haven't been out marching for rights you already have while dressed as a massive cunt.

But many activists criticised the march, pointing out that it focused largely on cisgender white women. 'What about African-American women with penises?' they cried. 'Why is no one going around with a black cock on their head?'

Katherine Nolan, the designer of the pussy-hat, withdrew the knitting pattern when she realised how offensive it was. 'I'm deleting the pattern I posted,' she said in a fittingly contrite statement. 'I am really sorry for upsetting people. I've read, listened and learned and while it was not intentional it was thoughtless. I will make some hats with yellow roses instead.'

The phrase 'too little too late' springs to mind. And has Nolan ever considered how triggering a yellow rose might be to anyone who has ever been raped by a florist?

I voted for Jeremy Corbyn reluctantly, because as an intersectionalist I would have preferred a black lesbian in the role. But there's always the possibility that Corbyn might transition at a later date, or that Diane Abbott might assume the Labour Party leadership and develop a taste for flange.

Corbyn has been dogged by accusations that his party is anti-Semitic, which I don't believe for one second. I've always loved Jews. I admire their caustic wit, their financial acumen and their cunning. And I have no doubt that Corbyn feels the same way.

Like all leftists, there is no place for anti-Semitism

in my life. I'm quite partial to the occasional bagel. I enjoy the songs of Barbra Streisand. I've even read that silly Anne Frank novel about a girl who gets stuck in a cupboard.

The British media have always mistrusted Corbyn, possibly because he doesn't seem to brush his hair very often. But it's simply untrue to suggest that he is a terrorist sympathiser. He stands accused of laying a wreath at the graves of Palestinian terrorists (if such a thing exists) who had murdered Israeli citizens, and then lying about it in a subsequent interview. But if somebody asked me to remember every single wreath I've ever laid I'm sure I'd struggle too.

Corbyn is woke as fuck, the unassailable rodeo cowboy riding bareback on the sturdy heifer of justice. He's pro BAME, pro LGBTQIA+, pro Islam, pro Irish republicanism, pro abortion, and respects women so much that he has called for them to have their own carriages on trains so that they can be protected from the terror that comes with male proximity. When Corbyn appeared at an event in Loughborough, white audience members were charged £10 more than ethnic minorities to hear him speak. The only thing that could have made the event more inclusive would have been to provide free rice and peas.

Labour is 'for the many, not the few', according to their current party slogan. The cover of their magazine at the 2018 party conference said it all, composed as it was of cartoons of various modern families. There were Asians, blacks, hijabis, a cripple, an interracial lesbian couple with their mixed-race child, a female construction worker, and even a ginger. Labour have moved on from all that tiresome 'class consciousness' that characterised the movement in the early to mid-twentieth century, and they are now the true bastions of identity politics.

The real reason why the media loathe Corbyn is that he represents a threat to the establishment. Socialism has been an unqualified success wherever it has been implemented. In Venezuela, at the time of writing, a 2.4-kg chicken is currently worth a whopping 14,600,000 bolivars.

So much for socialism making people poorer.

Ode to a Homeless

Capitalism took your home,
Stole your rooves to erect its shrines of avarice,
Tossed you gutterly into vagabondish slums
Like a buckstopped empress roughly licked.

Your blankets were purloined by a filofaxed terrorist
With a rusty corkscrew for a phallus,
Spinfucking his way into semi-pregnant souls
As a goatish spatula of ire, ever stirring.

Neoliberalism is a hairy sandwich
Half-nibbled by a cobbler's second arse,
An elongated musk that drenches the reasty air
Like curdled tofu from a grumpy fridge.

But the masses shall ascend,
A thousand armour-plated Lily Allens,
To batterslap the sharpsuited toothtwisters
As they gallivant on a shit-smudged trampoline of fear.

Meghan

She markled her way
    into the heart of a beige changeling.
Sinuous in Givenchy fatigues,
    She writhes,
        deadly,
A crispy buglocked fetterwitch in white.

Commoners swarm,
    yielding their throats,
Limbless lice in a shrill soufflé
    As she clings
        Limpet-like
        To a ginger scrotum, royally.

You ain't no goddam feminist.
    A foxtrotting mule of heteronormativity
Beckons the Beckhams to a champagne-sucking scumfest.
    It was the owl that shrieked,
    'Hewitt, to woo.'
That's the fatal bellman, bitch.

I Am Womxn

My front hole is tethered to the past,
A fraying ligature of blubbering lust
Cordtightened into a gilded ghoul
Who suckles the jostling buggertrain of lies,
For I am womxn.

I have crowdfunded my right to scream,
Stampeding gently on a three-backed beast
I howl at the universe through a miasma
Of upskirting scatterqueens on plump stilts.
Yes, I am womxn.

Drowned in my own ink,
A meaty pirouette of hangdog pickpocketry.
My breasts are syphilitic hoglets,
Delicate cross-eyed hymns of cheese.
See, I am womxn.

Genocide is orgasm made flesh,
This sneering glut of gnarled delinquency.
An onyx ashtray for a heart,
My bric-a-brac joy stubbed out in cold ashes.
Lo, I am womxn.

In the tepid dreams of a slutshamed goat
I am fingered by a god called Choice,
A beardless embryo serenading
Through the dim grey secrets of the night.
I am womxn.

Dead Fairies and Front Holes

'Woman' and 'man' are figures of male speech. Gender
– no less than sexuality – is an irreducible fiction.
David M. Halperin

We should give all newborn babies numbers
rather than names until they are ready to
determine their own gender identity.

This is an idea that I have floated through various
mediums: political pamphlets, slam poetry, interpret-
ative dance, shaman pottery and an online petition
entitled 'Some babies are trans: get over it'.

One sign that a baby is uncomfortable in its own
body is if it is crying on a regular basis. If, say, you
have given it a male name and dressed it in blue, it
may well be that its tears are an indicator of gender
dysmorphia. If the crying persists after a month or so,
you should seriously consider hormone blockers.

It's never too early to implement such procedures,
even if the person in question is still a foetus. I would
advise all pregnant mothers to be vigilant. If they can
feel their unborn child kicking, this is probably

99

because it is attempting to signal a desire to transition.

There are some who have the audacity to suggest that transitional medication for a child is a form of abuse. These people would sooner an individual grow up in the wrong body than administer a few harmless injections to thwart the tyranny of nature. Who's the real abuser here?

I mention all of this because enlightened society now realises that gender is fluid, the outdated categories of 'male' and 'female' being dictatorial taxonomies assigned randomly at birth. Some 'experts' still maintain that there are only two sexes. The idea that knowledge is more important than feelings is everything that is wrong with the field of modern science.

To put it simply, we are all transgender; it's simply a matter of extent. I am sick of people disputing my point of view on this issue and will no longer tolerate it. 'Debate' in such circumstances amounts to a form of mass murder, because it involves a denial of the existence of trans bodies. It's like J. M. Barrie says in *Peter Pan*: 'Every time a child says, "I don't believe in fairies," there is a fairy somewhere that falls down dead.'

Yet we are all forced to comply with the stale old dichotomy of male and female every time we fill out an application form for a new job, complete a survey or even apply for a bank account. There are a few major companies who are doing their best to coax our society into the twenty-first century. HSBC, for instance, is currently offering the choice of ten gender-neutral titles for its customers: Mx, Ind, M, Misc, Mre, Msr, Myr, Pr, Sai and Ser. There are still more titles I would like to see represented, including (but not limited to): Mg, Mrg, Qx, Ug, Ct, Fk, Wk, Bs, Pnky and Prky.

Facebook has also updated its policies on gender, now offering its users in excess of seventy different options. So instead of ticking the box for 'male' or 'female' or 'other', you can select from a whole host of identities such as 'demiman', 'demiwoman', 'polygender', 'multigender', 'genderqueer', 'transmasculine' or 'two-spirit'. But the fact that the number of gender options is only in double digits reveals just how much more work still needs to be done.

'Ah well,' the detractors cry, 'some people claim to be Napoleon; should we indulge them as well?' To which I always reply: yes. If someone identifies as Napoleon, they are Napoleon. I could elaborate on this principle, but I resent the idea that I should enact that labour in order to satisfy the demands of reactionaries.

I find it disgusting that the principle of self-identification is so roundly mocked by tabloid chauvinists. Rod Liddle, for instance, wrote a sneering article for the *Sunday Times* entitled 'I'm identifying as a young, black, trans chihuahua, and the truth can go whistle'. I cannot condemn him enough for his dismissive and unfeeling stance.

Unless he's being serious, in which case I offer him my warmest congratulations.

One of my favourite new terms is 'otherkin'; a person who identifies as non-human. By this I don't mean those who do not obviously resemble the archetypal human form, such as Barry Manilow or Janet Street-Porter, but rather those who know deep in their souls that they are beyond the scope of mere *homo sapiens*.

In order to be truly woke, one must also be ready to adopt a range of differently gendered pronouns, which can vary from individual to individual. The traditional pronouns of 'she' and 'he' are deployed so thoughtlessly, and involve a shocking degree of prejudice. Note, for instance, that historians tend to refer to King Henry VIII as a 'he'. But why? Do they ever stop to think that Henry might have preferred a nonconformist pronoun? There is nothing particularly male about having a huge beard, broad shoulders and a massive cock. My friend Belinda is hung like a shire stallion. That doesn't make her any less feminine.

It takes very little effort to learn someone's pronouns, or to announce your own. Many universities across the UK issue badges during freshers' week for this very purpose, so you can immediately see when it is appropriate to use she/her/her, he/him/his, they/them/their, xe/xem/xyr, ne/nym/nis, ne/nem/nir, ae/aer/aers, ve/ver/vis, ey/em/eir, fae/faer/faers, shey/shem/sheir, per/per/pers, tey/ter/tem, ze/hir/hir, zhe/zhim/zhers or zie/zim/zir. What could be simpler than that?

One of the highlights of my year is International Pronoun Day on 17 October when, as the University of Wisconsin's Lesbian Gay Bisexual Transgender Resource Center puts it, we can all help to 'transform society to celebrate people's multiple, intersecting identities'. Of all the problems that the global community faces today, surely this has to take priority. I can envisage no better way to celebrate diversity than to shun those bigots who refuse to learn the correct terminology, to enforce the use of multiple neopronouns through robust hate speech laws, and to seek out dissenters and punish them without mercy. It's what Mahatma Gandhi would have done if xe were alive today.

I would rather be shot by a lone wolf terrorist than be misgendered.

The criminalisation of non-woke language is just the beginning. The next step is to ensure that nobody's feelings are ever hurt by the assumption of gender. To this end, many secondary schools in the UK are currently in the process of introducing gender-neutral uniforms and prohibiting girls from wearing typical 'female' clothing. For a trans person, the sight of a skirt is likely to trigger major anxiety. If we simply jettison all obvious appearances of traditional gender distinctions, then everyone will be happy. And if you're one of those people who wouldn't be content under such circumstances, then you probably don't deserve happiness in the first place.

Many trans people oppose these innovations, claiming that it is patronising for cis individuals such as myself to advocate on their behalf for special protections. This kind of internalised transphobia breaks my heart, and if anything simply proves the necessity to introduce such measures. I know what is best for the trans community, even if they don't know it themselves.

We need to rethink our entire approach to this subject, and the best way would be to introduce Gender Studies to the national curriculum. Children need to understand that vaginas, penises, ovaries, testes and fallopian tubes are all mere social constructs. It is essential that we teach them that the very concept of gender is a fabrication, but is simultaneously the most essential aspect of their self-identity.

Calling out the misuse of language is a pivotal aspect of this struggle. A San Franciscan medical information service called Healthline recently published an 'LGBTQIA safe sex guide', which has embraced more appropriate terms for human genitalia. For instance, whenever a reference to what is conventionally known as a 'vagina' is required, the writers of the guide use the term 'front hole'.

The great thing about the phrase 'front hole' is not only that it's inclusive, but it's also much sexier than 'vagina'. After all, 'vagina' is Latin for 'sheath'.

I am no man's sheath.

This wonderful move towards greater inclusivity inspired me to write my first full-length play, *The Front Hole Monologues*, which I performed at my local fringe theatre. Critics were unanimous in their praise. 'Shockingly literal in its execution', wrote the

Lincoln Courier. 'McGrath seems wholly oblivious to nuance or taste', said the *Stage*. My favourite was the review in *TheatreBlogUK*, which simply asked: 'What the fuck did I just watch?'

Islamofeminism

Prophet Muhammad was not only a feminist for his time, but also an intersectional feminist who wanted to generate as much inclusivity as possible.

Muslim Girl Magazine

In order to achieve wokeness, one must treat Muslims with special sensitivity. This is essential given the increasingly vehement forms of prejudice they face due to damaging stereotypes in the media and popular culture, as well as legitimate grievances in Islamic communities, which have arisen as a direct corollary of Western depredations in international conflicts.

Also, some of them have bombs.

I am not for one moment trying to play down the terrible impact of terrorist atrocities. I despise ISIS. They're the sort who give Islamic fundamentalism a bad name; a group so repugnant that the writers of the television drama *Downton Abbey* had to kill off the family dog, also called Isis, because the name had become tarnished. Personally, I find it more likely that

ISIS changed their name to ISIL in case people started thinking they were fans of *Downton Abbey*.

But here's a thought. If a sufficient number of feminists were to join ISIS, we could turn it into a progressive social justice movement.

Every time I hear about another act of jihadist terrorism my heart sinks because I know there'll be a horrible Islamophobic backlash. Whatever their crimes, nothing that ISIS have ever done comes close to the acts perpetrated by the European nations during the Crusades. Surely in the face of modern-day jihadism, we need to be focusing on the misdeeds of medieval Christians. Anything else would be sheer hypocrisy.

And it's not as though matters have improved over time. Remember when that Christian bakery in Belfast refused to make a cake for a gay customer with the message 'Support Gay Marriage'? Westerners have to get their own house in order before they start criticising the more excessive behaviour of a few radical Islamists.

According to the theory of intersectionality, Muslims occupy the very pinnacle of the victim hierarchy. This is largely a consequence of the fact that they have been scapegoated continuously ever since 9/11. The irony is that we can't even be sure that Muslims were responsible. Those men could have been Quakers in disguise for all we know.

Some right-wingers like to pretend that there is a contradiction between the tenets of Islam and fourth-wave feminism. But if they actually spent some time in Pakistan or Saudi Arabia or any of the world's other Islamic states, they would realise that attitudes towards women are extremely progressive. To prove it, later this year I'll be organising a slut-walk through the centre of Karachi.

If there's really a problem with gender inequality in predominantly Muslim countries, how do you explain that there has never been a single successful conviction in a Sharia court for misogynistic hate crime?

Checkmate, motherfuckers.

'What about gay rights?' the Islamophobes scream, completely ignorant of the multitude of queer Muslims out there. Admittedly there are many who are still in the closet, such as the radical hook-handed cleric Abu Hamza, but that is to be expected given the homophobia that still pervades modern British society. Even in territories dominated by ISIS, gay people are known to happily shout it from the rooftops.

There is no genuine inconsistency between gay rights and Islam. Yes, the majority of British Muslims believe that homosexuality should be illegal, but if gay people simply abstain from sex during Ramadan this strikes me as a workable compromise.

'What about free speech?' the bigots bellow in rage, often quoting Muslims out of context to imply that they oppose individual liberty. Take the case of Pakistani pop star Rabi Peerzada, who caused outrage when she apparently called for the execution of French cartoonists who had drawn the Prophet Muhammad.

'Freedom of expression can never justify blasphemy,' she tweeted. 'Making blasphemy cartoon of Prophet is the worst act of terrorism. The Sketch makers must be hanged immediately.'

Some people (i.e. racists) petitioned Twitter to have Peerzada banned. Of course, they hadn't taken into account the postscript to her tweet – اور ہماری زبان میں – لکھ لعنت کتے کی شکل والے پر۔ – which I think is Urdu for 'LOL, only kidding, that would be mental'.

Westerners have to understand that there is a civil war raging within Islam, and moderates are trying to reform the more problematic beliefs. We could see evidence of this when Islam was rebranded as The Religion Of Peace™, which I think we can all agree is much catchier. This also helps to remind everyone that when somebody drives a truck into a group of pedestrians, shouting 'Allahu Akbar', it has absolutely nothing to do with Islam.

Then there is the question of the veil, opposition to which is surely one of the most blatant forms of Islamophobia imaginable. For instance, many have complained about Marks and Spencer's range of hijabs for schoolgirls as young as three, but surely the last thing we'd want to see is small children dressed as raging whores.

Even better, these tiny hijabs are very reasonably priced at only £6 each, and are available in a variety of colours from black to very black.

There has been much made in the press recently of women in Iran who are risking arrest by dancing in public and refusing to cover their hair as a form of protest. One woman was sentenced to two years in prison when footage of her removing her hijab was shared widely on social media. But as Western feminists such as Linda Sarsour will tell you, the hijab is a symbol of empowerment. Sharia law, Sarsour informs us, is 'reasonable' and 'makes a lot of sense'.

So just what do these Iranian protesters think they are doing? Do they have any idea how difficult they are making it for Western feminists to smash the patriarchy? Just cover your fucking hair, bitches.

I'm not saying that women who refuse to wear the veil deserve to be imprisoned, but they don't *not* deserve it either.

Thankfully, some brave Muslim women are fighting back, and are donning the hijab, the burka and the niqab as feminist symbols. Recently, beauty queen Sara Iftekhar broke new ground by wearing a hijab in the final of the Miss England competition. She had already been voted the most attractive woman in Huddersfield, which admittedly is a bit like winning an arm wrestle in a hospice. Nevertheless, the fact that Iftekhar didn't feel able to wear the full burka in the final reveals just how Islamophobic these 'beauty contests' really are.

It is up to our politicians to take charge of this desperate situation and make any criticism of Islam a hate crime punishable in accordance with Sharia law. It is perfectly possible to be a liberal who supports censorship and anti-blasphemy legislation.

Theresa May, for all her faults, has shown her support by quoting from the Koran at the Conservative Party conference because, although she isn't a Muslim herself, she is an amateur imam in her spare time.

But the former Foreign Secretary, Boris Johnson, inflamed interfaith relations when he compared Muslim women in burkas to letterboxes. Only the very next day I saw our postman delivering letters to our local mosque, which I presume was meant as some kind of sick joke. Words have consequences.

Johnson's offensive analogy inspired hordes of youths across the country to terrorise Muslims with envelopes. One Twitter user, Amanda Fleiss, wrote: 'I've just seen a Burka wearing Muslim lady with her kids being abused outside the medical centre, youths were shoving envelopes in her face, and her kids were crying. Police had to be called. This is your doing Boris Johnson.'

I am sickened that there are people out there who think this anecdote might be made up. And even if it is, it tells us more about modern British society than a thousand 'true' stories ever could.

The World Must Not Be Peopled

Inter faeces et urinam nascimur.
St Augustine of Hippo

We need to talk about unpaid labour.

There are literally thousands of married women who spend a good deal of their finite lives on this planet attending to their offspring. This is, to put it bluntly, a waste of fucking time. But more to the point, they are not being remunerated in any way for this most arduous of responsibilities.

If women choose to sacrifice the prospect of a career in order to breed, that is of course up to them. By doing so, however, they are embodying all that is rotten in patriarchal society. They have internalised their misogyny to such a degree that they genuinely believe that raising a child is more important and rewarding than earning money.

They hate women. They hate themselves. They are worse than men.

For the sake of balance, I should concede that some women are instinctively attracted to the idea of

113

propagation. This isn't something that I've ever fully understood, but I am far too tolerant by nature to rush to any judgement.

Some of my friends tell me that being a parent is one of life's most fulfilling tasks, and that childbirth itself is a beautiful miracle. So, by all means, if you wish to have some freeloading homunculus gestating inside you for nine months, only to tear its way free in the kind of gory spectacle that wouldn't look out of place in an *Alien* movie, be my guest.

Children are needy, they lack basic social skills and are unable to assist with any kind of serious manual labour. I have little to no patience with those who are not my intellectual equivalents, and so the only time I can ever bring myself to associate with children is when I am educating them in social justice. I consider this a moral duty, albeit a wearisome one. Twice a week I spend an hour at my local primary school, teaching the kids about period poverty or the evils of corporate capitalism, or explaining to them why gender is a destructive fiction.

Sometimes I run workshops for the younger pupils in which I help them to develop their skills in the realm of political slam poetry. My work genuinely seems to resonate with the more intelligent among them, particularly 'Humpty Dumpty was a Racist Fuck', 'Ozymandias Part 2', 'Cher's Spare Exoskeleton', 'Butternut Squash is Sexist' and 'Peppa Pig's Second Favourite Dildo'.

All heterosexual intercourse is rape. Ergo, all fathers are rapists. There is nothing remotely woke about having children. It is a grotesque and entirely unnecessary biological function. If the Darwinists are right, and flawed traits are eventually eliminated through a process of natural selection, it won't be long before the human species has evolved beyond the undignified urge to reproduce. Our sexual organs are really no different from our appendix; just a hangover from a primitive time when we lived in caves and ate grass.

In a sense, I sometimes think that King Herod had the right idea. Babies are overrated and eminently disposable. I am not, of course, inciting anyone to commit acts of murder (this I must emphasise for legal reasons), I am simply noting that many of society's problems could be alleviated if we relaxed the laws on infanticide.

Those who argue for the so-called 'continuation of the human race' are missing two key points. Firstly, why are women overwhelmingly shouldering this grave existential burden? Secondly, given the fact that we live in an irrepressibly misogynistic society, is the human race really worth preserving?

But if some women are to insist on taking responsibility for their own children, the least that the government can do is to pay them properly for their work. Why should a woman be expected to clean, clothe and feed their own child if there's no cash incentive? Particularly if that child is male.

My friend Tabitha has recently given birth to a baby boy. We both had our fingers crossed for non-binary, but an early ultrasound revealed the ghastly truth.

After the birth, one of the very first things this organism did was cry to be fed. That's the kind of male entitlement we're dealing with here. Straight out the womb, and it's all 'me, me, me'. Tabitha's son really is a nauseating piece of shit.

But of course giving birth to a daughter presents its own particular set of difficulties. As Simone de Beauvoir famously remarked, 'one is not born, but rather becomes a woman'. The truth of this is indubitable. Nobody's ever given birth to an adult woman, for fuck's sake. It seems odd that it needed to be pointed out in the first place.

Then there are the societal pressures to consider. Babies are not immune to everyday sexism. When my niece was born, my brother and his wife sent me a card which read: 'Baby Alison arrived on 2nd July 2017, 8 pounds 4 ounces'. The girl had only been alive for a few days and already her parents were fat-shaming her.

I return to my point about the morality of procreation in a misogynistic world. To those women who feel broody, I say this. Every sperm is an invader. It seeks to wriggle its way into your body, to penetrate your very soul, to filch all your potential for the sake of a bawling sprog who will only grow up to resent you. If the sperm is the bullet, then the phallus is the machine gun.

Live for yourself, not for an unborn parasite.

Toxic Masculinity

'It's a boy!'
Cries the doctor,
His tombstone tongue clacking
Like a forked phallus
In a dead donkey's quim.

My baby has bollocks for eyes.
Its body a slippery, bloodshot thicket of male flesh,
Wriggling, retching, screwing itself into my psyche.
This cuckoo brewed within my sacred space,
Only to rip-rape its way out into the world.

'Fuck you, bitch,' the notgirl whispers
Through a predatory milkman smile,
Sniggerburning my skin with its toxicity,
As it fashions a patriarchal noose
From the pubic hair of a thousand weeping midwives.

Every baby boy is an abomination,
A savage nugget of pus scooped from an open wound
And dumped into sullied uteri.
Mothers are cuckstumped cradlers of newborn men,
Spitsticked petticoats drenched in broiling cum.

Menstruators

We bleed
    Like florets of pity, deadened into burly clams
Twice solely gobbletossed by a scrumping leper
    As beefcurtained strap-on dreams of selfhood
Wrench the damaged crablouse
       from its hairy home.

Happyfat in fuck-me plimsolls   I roll
    Gardencentred by a spermatozoon called Fate
The singsong dingdong of a monthly rendezvous as
      We bleed
    With unfurled treason dripdripdrip red.

    Wrinkled and twatsauced
We bleed
Brazen like leaking sirens,
Finflapping on an unknown shore,
    Calling to cocksure sailors with throbbing
      thumbs.

    A rayon bullet soaked in power,
An orgy of dying sprats inside a makeshift scrotum.
    Gorging ourselves on oestrogen dreams
We bleed
    Like a slapped niece earmuffed by retarded
      camels
And slutwalking into the timid jaws of death.

A Vegan's Lament

In the abattoir of eternity
Goats cluster, corpsehooved
Into blood-sluiced tessellations
Of the incessantly milked.

I ruminate on ruminants,
A generation of innocent boycows
Lost to the porkbeefing folly
Of slackjawed mammal-noshers.

Hotdogs are coffins
Wherein pigs are sausaged into
Genocidal pipettes of futility,
Delivering oblivion to savage mouths.

What of the noble egg,
Ovoid locket of the unchickened,
Scrambled and desecrated
On a toasty deathbed?

And what of the stately ewe,
Primped and fluffy on a hillock,
Her destiny to be shredded
And strewn amidst a disappointing goulash?

In my dreams I hear them still,
The cud-chewers with halal haloes.
A thousand boltgunned heifers
Moo for vengeance.

Freeze Peach

Free speech is a fundamental foundation of a free and fair democracy. But let's be honest and have the guts to unpick who gets to speak, where, and why.

Reni Eddo-Lodge

Imagine thinking that free speech meant that people can say whatever they want, whenever they want. That's exactly how Nazi Germany started.

As *Guardian* columnist Owen Jones has pointed out, the phrase 'free speech' is 'nothing more than a political ploy, a ruse, a term the far right wilfully abuse to spread hatred'. And it isn't just left-wing journalists such as Jones who have reached this conclusion. Many intelligent and charismatic people feel this way too.

To live in a truly free society, there must be limits on individual forms of verbal expression. My guiding principle, which has served me very well for all my twenty-four years on this grubby male-ridden planet, is that those who to try to defend free speech are invariably crypto-fascists. These are the kind of people who miss the racist 'good old days' and like to say the word 'mongoloid', which is incredibly offensive to the spastic community.

Besides, free speech is selective. When I performed my poem 'God and Other Pederasts' at my local library's over-sixties reading club, I was asked to leave. Apparently they found my miming 'obscene and distressing'.

That was the whole fucking point. Philistines.

Free speech extremists are forever complaining about 'PC culture' or that they are constantly 'treading on eggshells'. As I've pointed out many times before, this figure of speech is a microaggression towards vegans and should not be tolerated.

Nobody is going to prevent anyone from saying the right things, so it stands to reason that the only people who require free speech are those who are planning on saying the *wrong* things. If it weren't for free speech, Pol Pot wouldn't have been able to order the death of a single Cambodian.

The best take on this issue has come, inevitably, from that celebrated scholar Laurie Penny:

> *I am done pretending that the good intentions of white patriarchy are more important than the consequences enacted on the bodies of others. Good intentions aren't the issue here. Feel free to be as racist as you like in the privacy of your own heart, if you can live with yourself, but not – and this is very important – in the privacy of your own house.*

The question Penny leaves unanswered is how this policy is to be enforced. Agents of the GDR found a solution after the Second World War, which was to bug the houses of citizens. There is no doubt that we should follow suit.

Think about it. People are *far* more likely to say offensive things if they think nobody's listening.

Censorship is an important tool of any government in order to guarantee our freedoms. The data would seem to suggest that we are moving steadily in the right direction, caught in the soothing tractor beam of wokeness. According to the Pew Research Center, 40 per cent of young people in the USA would support government censorship of 'statements that are offensive to minority groups'. And in the UK, hate speech laws are being enacted with greater regularity in order to clamp down on problematic opinions and distasteful comedy. Markus Meechan was convicted in a court of law for uploading a video to the internet in which he is seen teaching a pug to give a Hitler salute. He claimed that this was a joke, but of course there is nothing remotely amusing about a Nazi pug.

The video was viewed three million times, and I shudder to think how many impressionable dogs were radicalised by this spectacle before YouTube eventually took it down.

Recently, police in the UK have been petitioning the general public to 'report non-crime hate incidents', which would incorporate 'offensive or insulting comments, online, in person or in writing'. In this new woke era, our law enforcement agencies are not content to police crime, but also non-crime. This is a huge relief, because for a long while now too many citizens have been not breaking the law and getting away with it.

Postmodernists have explained time and time again that language is the basis of reality. Nothing is authentically true beyond the discourse through which it is conveyed. This is why there were no homosexuals before the word was coined in 1868, no alcoholics before the first diagnosis in 1849, no Galápagos tortoises before they were discovered in 1535, and no electricity before it was invented in 1879.

With this in mind, it seems obvious that in order to defeat bigotry, we only need to eradicate the words required to express bigoted views.

Let's try a quick thought experiment. Picture, if you will, a homophobic man. There is some hate speech brewing inside his mind, ready to erupt. Perhaps he wishes to express the sentiment, 'I disagree with same-sex marriage.' But the words do not exist. They were outlawed decades ago and are no longer in currency. What would our man do then?

The answer is obvious. He would sit there in an embarrassed silence, until eventually coming around to the idea that actually there's nothing he'd enjoy more than to fellate another man to the strains of 'YMCA'.

Student unions at universities are currently spearheading the battle against free speech through the creation of 'safe spaces' where debate is outlawed if the topics are potentially triggering. At Oxford, a debate on abortion was cancelled because a man with incorrect views was scheduled to appear. Debates are all very well in principle, but there's no need to represent all sides of an argument. One protestor, Niamh McIntyre, said, 'The idea that in a free society absolutely everything should be open to debate has a detrimental effect on marginalised groups.' A university is hardly the appropriate place for exploring alternative ideas.

This is why higher education institutions must strive to decolonise their curricula in order to amplify new diverse voices and dismantle the toxic male whiteness of history. The likes of Dostoyevsky, Newton and Schopenhauer should be dispatched to oblivion. It is now clear that they contributed very little to our culture in the first place.

The same goes for the Ancient Greeks; a bunch of misogynistic dead white males who only ever valued free speech as a means to denigrate women. 'By speech,' wrote the orator Isocrates, 'we educate the ignorant and inform the wise.' I can't be the only person to have noticed that the phrase 'inform the wise' is an anagram of 'feminist whore'.

Fuck you, Isocrates. Your time is over.

The Androcaust

The proportion of men must be reduced to and maintained at approximately 10% of the human race.

Sally Miller Gearhart

In 1610, a white male 'poet' whose name isn't worth mentioning wrote a play called *Cymbeline*. In the second act, one of his many two-dimensional characters asks the question: 'Is there no way for men to be, but women must be half-workers?'

In John Milton's *Paradise Lost*, Adam laments the creation of his wife Eve in a similar fashion. 'O why did God,' he asks, 'not fill the world at once with men' and 'find some other way to generate mankind?'

This is the fantasy that lurks in the stygian hearts of all males: a utopian vision of a future in which all women are eliminated, concupiscent urges are fulfilled by obedient sex robots, and reproduction can be achieved without the need of female involvement.

For most men, sex with a woman is simply an alternative form of masturbation. To put it bluntly, women are considered no more than wank-socks for their seed. So it is inevitable that men should secretly harbour a desire to procreate on their own, much like amoebas. It's an appropriate analogy, given that an amoeba and a human male share a similar degree of intellectual nous. As the character of Val says in Marilyn French's novel *The Women's Room*, 'all men are rapists, and that's all they are'.

I do not hate men. I pity them. They are lesser creatures, anencephalous dicks with dicks who have been taught from birth that they are the commanders of the universe. It's a kind of culturally enforced mass delusion. If you train a dog to lick a plate, that doesn't make it a washing machine.

They say that you should fight fire with fire. This is typical male logic, because actually if you set fire to a burning house it achieves very little. If you take this advice as metaphorical, however, there is something to be said for attack being the best means of defence. And if I am right about the ubiquitous male fantasy to rid the world of women, it stands to reason that we should get there first.

To avoid the possibility of any ambiguity, I'll just come out and say it. This is an idea that came to me all of a sudden while I was contemplating my state of permanent subjugation, last summer on a brief skiing trip to Val d'Isère.

It is simply this. *The time of men is over. The next step is their wholesale elimination.*

So how do we go about it? For a while there on Twitter, #KillAllMen was trending worldwide, until the despots who run the company decided that this was 'inflammatory' and started banning accounts who dared to use it.

I am not a fan of murder. In many cases it is considered illegal, and personally speaking, on balance, I think it is generally a bad thing. It's right up there with mansplaining and the government's tax on tampons.

So when I suggest that we should 'kill all men', I am not talking about murder as such. I am talking about modifying our society so that, over a period of time, the very existence of males will be consigned to the history books.

Allow me to explain. If gender is culturally determined (which it is) then there is no sound reason for *anyone* to identify as male at all. It is only because we live under such a tyrannous oppressive patriarchy that roughly half of the population accept the 'male' label with which they were assigned at birth. Once our society embraces the eternal feminine, there will be no need for its vile opposite. Yin will have swallowed yang. The rattlesnake will have severed its deadly tail. The whetted spoon of femininity will have cracked the hairy shell of truth.

There are perks to being male, granted. Men are paid much more than women for the same work, they rarely have to queue for toilets and they are statistically less likely to fall pregnant.

But we shouldn't overestimate these differences, as to do so would be to fall into the trap of biological essentialism. We've all heard the myths: men are more aggressive, men enjoy football and beer, men have penises, etcetera. But these are simply roles that certain members of the human race are encouraged to play.

Some say, for instance, that only men are able to urinate while standing up. To prove them wrong, I only *ever* urinate standing up, and it's extremely liberating. I would urge all women to do the same so that we can finally break down these deleterious stereotypes. (Although you should have some kitchen roll to hand as it can get rather messy.)

The Amazons lived plentiful lives without men. They were a race of warriors who were so badass that they removed one of their breasts in order to better facilitate the use of a bow and arrow. Would a male soldier sacrifice a testicle for their cause? Unlikely.

This explains why the word 'Amazon' comes from the Classical Greek *a*- (ἀ-) and *mazos* (μαζός), which is best translated as 'without breast'. The word was famously appropriated by the online bookseller of the same name. Amazon's founder, Jeff Bezos, claims that he made the choice because it sounded 'exotic and different', whereas I suspect that he was attracted to the word's etymology. How perfect that the name of a corporate trillion-dollar tech giant run by a predominantly male board of directors literally means 'No Breasts'.

If you don't believe that an all-female world is practicable, you should read *Herland* by Charlotte Perkins Gilman. First published in 1915, this farsighted novel depicts an idealised society in which all the trappings of toxic masculinity – war, aggression, competitive belching – are but distant memories. There is not a scrotum in sight.

Gilman is best known for her short story 'The Yellow Wallpaper' (1892), but *Herland* takes her out of the traditionally feminine realm of interior design and into the male-dominated genre of utopian science-fiction. To me, *Herland* is more than just a novel. It's a guidebook. It's a prophecy of a better world.

Let's make it happen.

Clockwork Fascists

We are all HIV-positive.
Diamanda Galás

When it comes to promoting equality, Hollywood plays a vital role. We all take our cues from popular culture; our behaviour is almost entirely dictated by the films and television shows we enjoy. This is known as 'media effects theory', and even though six decades of research have failed to produce any evidence for it, my lived experience confirms that it is true.

There have always been movies that combat fascism and champion wokeness. Frodo and Sam in the *Lord of the Rings* series did wonders for LBGT awareness by showing that even hobbits could be sodomites. And when Cy Endfield made his 1964 film *Zulu*, he insisted on casting numerous actors of colour.

One of the most successful franchises in history is, of course, *Star Wars*. The influence of these films can barely be overstated, but when it comes to representation they leave a lot to be desired. If Luke Skywalker had been cast as an aborigine back in 1977, racism would have been eliminated by now.

Then there is the question of sexual minorities. The paucity of LGBTQIA+ representation in the original *Star Wars* trilogy is clearly homophobic. As far as I can tell, there's only one lesbian character. She makes a brief appearance in *Return of the Jedi*, when Jabba the Hutt throws Luke Skywalker into her pit.

The most recent *Star Wars* films, which tend to come out every month or so, are being made by Disney, a mass media conglomerate that was founded by an American cartoonist who had his body frozen so that he could come back to life once all the Jews had gone.

These newer instalments are far more progressive than those made in the late seventies and early eighties. The writers of *Rogue One: A Star Wars Story* have noted that 'the Empire is a white supremacist (human) organisation' which is opposed in the film 'by a multi-cultural group led by brave women'. This is import-ant, because if works of fiction don't send a positive message about diversity, it's difficult to see what func-tion they serve. Movies exist to educate us, not to entertain. Orlando Bloom, for instance, has starred in a whole series of films in order to teach us that he has no discernible talent whatsoever.

I'm reminded of a quotation by the novelist Sabine Baring-Gould: 'God made most folks of clockwork and stuck them on their little plots of soil to spin round and run their courses, like the figures on an Italian barrel-organ.' We must accept that, for most people, free will is a myth. The working classes in particular are forever teetering on the brink of fascism. If we don't instruct them how to think and feel through the careful cultivation of popular culture, we risk nudging these malleable creatures into the abyss.

But it isn't just the movies that influence the behaviour of plebeians. Other forms of entertainment are also to blame for the current pandemic of Nazism sweeping our nation. It's been fifty years since the beloved sitcom *Dad's Army* was originally broadcast, but nobody has ever thought to ask why there were no women of colour in the cast. Why not?

Many feminists have argued that there need to be more strong female characters in television dramas. On the other hand, as screenwriter Daisy Goodwin has pointed out, by depicting women in powerful roles producers are guilty of 'airbrushing reality'. I would therefore like to see more shows in which women are depicted as powerful in order to send a positive message, but simultaneously depicted as weak in order to reflect the ways in which women are oppressed in society.

Comedy is another super-problematic area. Now I should say from the outset that I've never been interested in comedy. I haven't smiled since nursery school, and I regret that moment even now.

And why should I smile? Life is merely the shitty prelude to death.

Jokes are violence. This is because humour is a patriarchal construct, which explains why the stand-up industry has historically been so dominated by straight males, and a few gay ones here and there if they mince enough. As award-winning comedian Hannah Gadsby has said, stand-up is 'an art form designed by men for men'. Gadsby is at the forefront of a courageous new wave of feminist comics subverting the genre by ensuring that it doesn't make anyone laugh.

For too long, comedians have assumed that they can make light of anything and get away with it. Comedy needs to be purged of jokes that reinforce bigotry. Allow me to demonstrate:

When my wife and I argue we're like a band in concert: we start with some new stuff, and then we roll out our greatest hits.
> Frank Skinner (legitimising domestic violence)

West Mersea police announced tonight that they wish to interview a man wearing high heels and frilly knickers. But the Chief Constable said they must wear their normal uniforms.
> Ronnie Corbett (normalising transphobia or
> something)

I have a theory that Jordan married a cage fighter because she needed someone strong enough to stop Harvey from fucking her.
> Frankie Boyle (making the misogynistic
> assumption that a woman would be
> incapable of fending off her son
> without the help of her husband)

Reading over these 'jokes', it feels as though Hitler never died. It's clear that we urgently need to move into a new era of woke comedy, one that is carefully policed to ensure that all sensibilities are catered for. As Matt Zoller Seitz observed in an article for *Vulture*, straight white male performers will still be welcome, but they'll have to learn to listen 'when somebody calls them out on their subject matter, their joke writing, or their political opinions'. If these patriarchal comedians can't be bothered to self-censor in order to avoid perpetuating harmful stereotypes, then frankly they can suck my box.

Nica Burns, the director of the Edinburgh Comedy Awards, gave an impassioned speech to launch the 2018 festival fringe in which she said she was 'excited' by 'the woke movement, which is setting an ever-evolving agenda as it seeks to establish a clear marker for what is unacceptable today'. Such major figures in the comedy industry are right to insist on these parameters, and to remind us that the purpose of comedy is to educate the masses in matters of social decorum and the limits of free speech. If comedy is too humorous, this goal is unlikely to be achieved.

And it's not just comedians who will have to be reprogrammed. UK police officers have already been offered 'banter training' to combat the rise of problematic mirth. According to the workshop leaders, the course 'puts political correctness in its place, recognises the benefits of fun at work and focuses on the risks and responsibilities for all concerned'. Light-hearted jokes, if not properly regulated, can very quickly spiral out of control. Let's not forget that Al-Qaeda started off as an improvisational sketch group.

Ultimately, we all have a choice about what entertainment we consume, which in turn determines whether or not we can satisfy the prerequisites for wokeness. For instance, I only like music if it is produced by artists from marginalised groups. Def Leppard is a good example, because the drummer lacks an arm. Then there is Gabrielle, who is black, female and missing an eye. Lily Allen is another sound choice because she is clearly retarded.

Hip hop music is sublime, with the exception of white rap artists such as Eminem, Vanilla Ice and Pam Ayres. But while enjoying rap, one must guard against cultural appropriation. When Kendrick Lamar invited a white fan onto the stage to sing along to his song 'M.A.A.D City' at a concert in Alabama, he was forced to interrupt when she repeatedly used the n-word. Nobody can fathom why the girl indulged in this racist outburst. Some have surmised that it might have something to do with the word being a continual feature in the song's lyrics.

There can be no justification for whites using the n-word. One must have the necessary urban credentials before making proclamations such as 'Dayum nigga, dem wypipo be keepin' ma niggas down n' sheeit', which I believe is a quotation from Rachel Dolezal's autobiography.

I am all for artistic liberty, but when it comes to cultural appropriation, or causing offence to disenfranchised groups, I do maintain that art should be subject to a degree of censorship.

There's a simple formula. If it entertains, it's entertainment. If it offends, it's hate speech. It's up to the woke elite to supervise the boundaries.

Join us.

Comedy

Hatejokes spat into beseeching ears
As laughter downslams victimly
Onto frail heads triggered by
Non-nonbinary tyrants on a stage.
Haha is not my pronoun.

Punchlines are bayonets, severing throats
In a toxic chucklesmog of despair.
A homicidal mirth-whore speaks blood
And spills his surly mousse of ruination.
A second Rwanda.

With a 'knock knock' here
And a 'who's there' there,
The slapstick slopschtick in a shockjock slipstream.
Corpulent beavers rinse their sleeves
On the semi-skimmed tinsel of woe.

'It's just a joke,' the dagger shrieks
As it rapes the flesh of ad-libbed gaghags.
We are left broken and clownhumped
While chickens cross their roads
To fuck orphans with their gnarly beaks.

Mummy

You want a piece of me, Mummy?
Try my fibula, sharpened and thrust into your yawning
   heart.
I am wombed too buckly
To eat out a herd of quadrupeds,
Slippered grim by fate,
Prancing outwards within a glimmering hoop of offal.

I am a suicidal beacon of brainsoup.
Sunken, downtime for the pitchfork fingerprick
Tugging at the eunuch's scab with shitty pincers.
Mummy spreads my face
Across a leering lap of blood,
And stitches herself to an anvil of iniquity, tenfold.

Why do you keep that toffee apple in your hair,
   Mummy?
I did not consent
To be spunk-shunted into this world.
You had no right to murder me with life.
Mummy, Mummy,
Your soul is a dildo of hate.

I Am Titania McGrath

Titania,
Roaster of gammon,
With a flak-peppered parapet-chin, lofted.

Crypto-fascists tremble as I roar.
With gutpluck I steer the probing lance of virtue,
Like a laughing foreskin within a scarecrow's craw.

Valiant ecosexual Nazi-sniffer,
Swatting barbed words from cis-ethnic incubi
And brunching on the uber-problematic.

Through trolls with swastika smiles I crash,
The alpha female to a male omega,
A second Christ, a slay queen pioneer.

Androgynous blood flows; genderfluid.
The soy boy hoi polloi stiffen at my command
As slamdunk justice is dispensed with brio.

Spitting bees of love safespacely,
With a skullful of broken hearts I brawl,
Hornlocked and hyperwoke.

Conclusion

Ceci n'est pas une conclusion.
Titania McGrath

Reading over that last poem, I realise with a shudder that my work shall never be surpassed. Poetry ends with me.

Literally everything I do is art. I have a formidable gift. And yet this has its downsides. I find it tedious to be so constantly and consistently admired. As one sycophant recently said, 'William Blake was the Titania McGrath of his generation.'

It is true that some readers, mostly males, find it difficult to connect with my work. Very occasionally a woman will offer a criticism; a sad indictment of the now common phenomenon of internalised misogyny.

I am too dangerous for the literary establishment. I wield the truth like a sword, and we all know that (s)words can wound.

I am a healer, a weaver of dreams. I have been put on this earth to defend minorities and fight for social justice. My work is not about ego. It is so much bigger than me. This is why I would urge all my readers to spread the word about this book so as many copies as possible can be sold.

If you have made it through these pages then you have taken your first baby steps towards wokeness. But the patriarchy is a behemoth that will not be euthanised with ease. Only the other day I was out shopping for a birthday card for a feminist friend, and could find nothing that wasn't either pink or based upon traditionally feminine tastes. I had to go to three different stores before I found something suitable. How many more women have to be mildly inconvenienced before we make Gender Studies compulsory in schools?

As you try to change the world, you must prepare yourself for the predictable sneering from the ignorant and the unwoke. They will dismiss you as a 'social justice warrior', and accuse you of going out of your way to find things about which to be offended. When they do so, remind them that we live in a heteronormative patriarchy. *Everything* is offensive.

They will brand your views as 'Orwellian'. For this reason, it's a good idea to prepare yourself by studying George Orwell's most famous novel, *Nineteen Eighty-Four*. I recently read it for the first time, and was pleasantly surprised to find that the society depicted therein isn't quite the terrifying dystopia that everyone claims. There are some very sensible ideas, actually.

You must remember that bigotry is not always immediately apparent. We need to challenge the lazy assumption that people aren't racist just because they never say or do racist things. Unconscious bias is real. If you don't believe me, try applying for a job using a traditional black surname such as 'Mugabe'. See how far you get.

Unconscious bias against Muslims is particularly rampant. Studies show that 96 per cent of respondents would run away if they heard someone shouting 'Allahu Akbar' in a public place.

When it comes to racism, it can't simply be the responsibility of BAME people to reshape our white supremacist culture. If anything, it's the whites – the perpetrators of injustice – who should be agitating for change. Film star Anne Hathaway revealed herself to be a virtuous ally when she declared that 'all black people fear for their lives DAILY in America'. It's a distressing truth that needed to be articulated, and sometimes the opinions of all black people are best expressed by white celebrity millionaires.

The worst kind of prejudice is that which is subtle, and thereby all the more insidious. We've all got a friend who won't watch a film if it stars Cuba Gooding Jr, who can't spell Djibouti or who tuts at passing Sikhs. In the moment, such things seem trivial and unworthy of comment, but they can have a cumulative impact on social cohesion.

We need to be proactive. If you aren't a member of your local Antifa unit, you need to sign up. For those who don't know, 'Antifa' is an abbreviation of 'antifascist', which means they're allowed to punch people in the name of tolerance. As commentator Frank Guan has argued, the idea of social divisions being 'reconciled through "honest" conversation' is 'hopelessly outdated'. Much better to just hit someone over the head with a bike lock.

Antifa are at the forefront of this struggle. In years to come, the history books will record that our socialist utopia was achieved because of middle-class hipsters dressed up as the IRA, pepper-spraying Trump voters and shouting at Jacob Rees-Mogg.

So get involved. Make sure that you are setting the right example. This applies to your appearance as much as your conduct. You can begin by gaining weight. Being skinny is an act of violence. If you have a thin waistline you are, by definition, a bully. It's passive-aggressive fat-shaming. As *Huffington Post* reporter Michael Hobbes has argued in his article 'Everything You Know About Obesity Is Wrong', it is the stigma imposed upon the obese by doctors and the media that causes the most damage, rather than the fact that they can't brush their own teeth without wheezing.

Guard against comedians who mock the oppressed. Promote a new kind of woke culture, one in which comedy itself is eliminated. We should be taking our lead from Saudi Arabia, where satirists can be punished with jail sentences of up to five years. 'Satire' has long been a façade for spreading hate.

Make sure you are active online, because when it comes to recalibrating the zeitgeist social media is crucial. Let us not forget that ISIS has been all but defeated through a series of creative hashtags. As well as some late-night vigils with tealights, of course.

Take every opportunity to resist the plague of cultural appropriation. Racial boundaries must be strictly policed. Unlike gender, which is totally fluid.

Challenge your own lifestyle. If there are no women of colour in your immediate family, you need to be asking yourself: why not?

Call out privilege wherever it appears. It is surely no coincidence that it is only ever straight white men – the beneficiaries of structural privilege – who make assumptions about people based on their sexuality, race or gender.

And write to your MP. Demand that the state take a more dynamic involvement in curbing hate. The phrase 'free speech' is a racist dog whistle. The only way we can stop fascism is if the police are allowed to arrest people for what they say and think.

So what next for Titania McGrath? It has been an enjoyable experience sharing these thoughts, penning a kind of bible for my woke disciples. But I will not rest until we have achieved our diverse intersectional social-ist decolonised polyamorous genderqueer pro-trans body-positive anti-ableist privilege-checking speech-policing hate-free matriarchal utopia. There is still much work to be done as we wade together through the turbid waters of injustice.

I believe that I am at my most effective when I combine my art with my activism. After much consideration, therefore, I have decided that my next project will be to resolve the various conflicts in the Middle East through a short tour of my feminist slam poetry.

So if any of my readers know of any suitable venues in Mosul, Gaza or the Sistan–Baluchistan province, I would be grateful if they get in touch with my agent.

Community arts centres or vegan cafés work best.